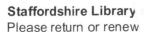

intrigued by tales of a g... and beyond the border. He couldn't have known then what Israel would come to mean to him, or foreseen the future occupation of his home in Palestine. Later, as a young lawyer, he worked to halt land seizures and towards peace and justice in the region. During this time, he made close friends with several young Jewish Israelis, including fellow thinker and searcher Henry. But as life became increasingly unbearable in the Palestinian territories, it was impossible to escape politics or the past, and even the strongest friendships and hopes were put to the test.

Brave, intelligent and deeply controversial, in this book award-winning author Raja Shehadeh explores the devastating effect of occupation on even the most intimate aspects of life. Looking back over decades of political turmoil, he traces the impact on the fragile bonds of friendship across the Israel–Palestine border, and asks whether those considered bitter enemies can ever come together to forge a common future.

WHERE
THE LINE
IS DRAWN

RAJA SHEHADEH

WHERE THE LINE IS DRAWN

Crossing Boundaries in Occupied Palestine

P

PROFILE BOOKS

First published in Great Britain in 2017 by
PROFILE BOOKS LTD
3 Holford Yard
Bevin Way
London
WC1X 9HD
www.profilebooks.com

1 3 5 7 9 10 8 6 4 2

Typeset in Aldus by MacGuru Ltd

Printed and bound in Great Britain by
Clays, Bungay, Suffolk

A CIP catalogue record for this book is
available from the British Library.

ISBN 978 1 78125 653 4
eISBN 978 1 78283 257 7

To the memory of my sister
Siham Shehadeh Baddour
(1946–2016)

Contents

The Stamp Collector

Ramallah, 1959

He looked too large for the cramped house. He always left his slippers under the bed, brought up his short stocky legs and folded them underneath him. It was only there on the bed, with its gleaming white sheet stretched over a large mattress, that he seemed to have enough room for his corpulent body.

This was the first house my parents and sister came to live in after they were forced out of Jaffa. How crowded it must have been.

I am eight years old and sprawled on the bed with my uncle. I occupy only a small space at one corner of the bed. His stamp collection is spread over the mattress – stamps of all sizes, large and small, squares and rectangles, with differently coloured serrated edges. Among them I see one with strange angular lettering. It looks ancient, pharaonic. I read the small Arabic script: Israel. When I point to it, my uncle puts his stubby finger to his mouth and whispers, 'Hush.' He turns his head to look around him, as if to see whether anyone has overheard us. Silently, I scrutinise the stamp more carefully. I am curious about the image on it. It is of an extended arm with strong fingers gripping an orange and white flower. What sort of body produces such a grip? I imagine broad shoulders and thick rippling muscles. Could that unreachable land be peopled by giants? There is writing on the side in Roman script, which I can't read. I ask my uncle to translate and he tells me it is French for 'the conquest of the desert'. I ask what conquest means and he explains.

I had of course heard of Israel, but I knew nothing about it other than what I had heard from my cousin Amal, who lived there, in Acre. Pointing to the hills next to our house – the only home I knew – she had once said, 'You see these hills that are brown? In Israel they would be all green.'

She and my aunt Mary, who spoke fast and was constantly puffing on a cigarette, were permitted to visit us, but just for a few days at a time. I never saw my male cousins because only women were allowed to cross the Green Line, the border until 1967 between Israel and Jordan – Jordan had annexed East Jerusalem and the West Bank in 1950. They seemed so wretched, their hair uncombed, their demeanour tense, demanding. Their visits were fleeting. They would come through the Mandelbaum Gate in Jerusalem to celebrate Christmas with us – not every year, only when they succeeded in getting a permit from the Israeli authorities. They never knew until the last minute whether or not they would be allowed to cross, and when they did, their visit would be so rushed they could hardly catch their breath. They were only allowed to stay for forty-eight hours. Then they would gather their things and whatever they had managed to buy – Turkish coffee cups were especially desirable – and they would leave as quickly as they had come. The house would then return to calm, and there would be lengthy discussions about them and their visit. Life in Israel seemed so difficult. We couldn't possibly envy them for living among hills that were greener than ours.

My uncle worked in Kuwait. I did not appreciate then what it meant to work in the desert without air conditioning. He said they had to sit in a barrel of cold water because it was so hot. To amuse himself in the desert he collected stamps.

He would rub his red eyes and then slowly pull the beautifully preserved stamps from between the transparent pages of his album. When he reached his most prized stamp, his eyes would open wide. He would hum and exhale slowly through pursed lips, taking his time as he slowly raised the stamp and held it up in front of my eyes. 'Now this one, this one is very precious,' he would say, and holding it carefully between the tips of his chubby fingers he would turn it round and gaze at it with admiration. 'But this one,' he would say, picking up the stamp from Israel, 'we must hide.'

Now, half a century later, having made countless crossings into the once forbidden land, I realise how unaware I had been at the time of what Israel would come to mean to me over the years. For nineteen years after the Catastrophe in 1948, or the Nakba, when around 750,000 Palestinians were forced out of their homes and Arab villages were razed to the ground with the end of the British Mandate and the establishment of Israel, we lived in the part of historic Palestine under Jordanian rule. How could we have known then that in a few years Israel would occupy our land, that over the years we would cross its borders so frequently and that our entire life would come to be dominated by the country with the unmentionable name?

2

Henry

Tel Aviv, 1977

He was short and stocky, with warm, intelligent eyes, thick hair and a fleshy nose. His face was round and his eyes sparkled above a bushy beard that seemed to mock the young face above it. He looked neither sinister, as people with beards sometimes do, nor like a sage. At first I didn't notice the beard, because his eyes captivated me with their freshness and purity. But it was hard to ignore. It looked as though he hadn't shaved for years – not even given it a trim. It was straggly, reaching almost to his waist. Maybe he was religious; perhaps he had made a vow.

His name was Henry Abramovitch.

It was 20 November 1977, a few months after my return from studying law in London, and I had accompanied my father to Tel Aviv, travelling through the olive groves of the West Bank, their silver leaves shimmering in the sun, down narrow, winding roads all the way to the coastal plain. We had driven along the old roads lined with eucalyptus trees to my father's city, Jaffa, and from there to Tel Aviv.

We had come to hear Anwar Sadat, the president of Egypt, address the Knesset. This was the first visit by an Arab leader to Israel. By then Israel and Egypt had fought four wars in under twenty years and Sadat was now boldly trying the path of peace.

We were there at the invitation of *New Outlook* magazine, a leftist Israeli publication to which my father contributed, and they had set up a large screen in the foyer of a hotel. It was the first time I had seen a TV projection on such a wide screen. As Sadat spoke, in Arabic, enunciating the words in his deep voice and thick Egyptian accent, I drank in everything he said – even his talk of religion, which for a cynical young man like me was unexpected:

> I come to you today on solid ground to shape a new life and to establish peace. We all love this land, the land of God. We all, Muslims, Christians and Jews, worship God ...
>
> Ladies and gentlemen, there are moments in the lives of nations and peoples when it is incumbent upon those known for their wisdom and clarity of vision to survey the problem, with all its complexities and vain memories, in a bold drive towards new horizons ... No one can build his happiness at the expense of the misery of others ...
>
> I have not come here for a separate agreement between Egypt and Israel ... There is no peace

that could be built on the occupation of the land
of others, otherwise it would not be a serious
peace … In all sincerity, I tell you that there
can be no peace without the Palestinians. It is a
grave error with unpredictable consequences to
overlook or brush aside this cause …

Here I tell you, ladies and gentlemen, that it is
no use to refrain from recognising the Palestinian
people – their right to statehood and their
right of return. We, the Arabs, have faced this
experience before with you, and with the reality
of Israeli existence, the struggle that took us from
war to war, from victims to more victims, until
you and we have today reached the edge of a
horrifying abyss and a terrifying disaster unless,
together, we seize this opportunity today of a
durable peace based on justice.

After over a decade of occupation by the Israelis,
who in 1967 had taken the West Bank, including East
Jerusalem, from Jordan in the June War, listening to
Sadat's speech gave me hope that perhaps we would
enter a new period of peace, that a new world was
beginning, that it was only a matter of time before
the occupation would end. I was exuberant. As soon
as Sadat had finished, I lost my father to his admirers
and the journalists who circled around him, wanting to
know what he thought. I remember his euphoric smile
as he moved from one group of men and women to
another while I sat alone and watched him. He was an
articulate, thoughtful man who had begun his career as

a lawyer in Jaffa in 1935 under the British Mandate. In 1948, during the Nakba, he lost his practice, his home and all his properties, and he had to start all over again in Ramallah. And yet he was a true believer in peace between the Palestinians and Israelis and thought that the peaceful coexistence of a Palestinian state side by side with an Israeli state would end years of enmity.

One of the consequences of the 1967 war was that very few of the friends I had grown up with were around. Either they had left with their families or they had gone to study abroad and never returned. I had to make new friends, and it was at this point in my life that the young, bearded man, Henry, sat down next to me and asked me what I thought of the speech. From his accent I could tell that he was Canadian.

I must have said something trite like: 'This will usher in huge political change.' At the time I was still under the impression that Israel needed our recognition and that it was we, the Palestinians, who were withholding it. I believed we held the power to resolve the conflict. Israel, which said it was ready to negotiate, supported that impression. They popularised it. And here was the head of the strongest Arab state offering Israel recognition.

Nevertheless, politics was not paramount in my mind – nor, as I discovered, was it in his. Henry, like me, was not political. I don't remember talking any more about Sadat's speech. Instead, we discussed identity, how Israel had succeeded in forging a national identity and Palestine had not. The Nakba had effectively dismantled Palestinian society.

Henry

At the time I was searching for an identity. Jordan, since assuming control of the West Bank in 1948, had tried to suppress Palestinian culture and identity and turn us Palestinians into loyal subjects of Jordan's Hashemite king. Whatever history we were taught glorified the role of the Hashemites, who originated from Arabia and had led the revolt against the Ottoman Empire. I knew from my home education that I was not Jordanian. I had also heard of Jordan's shameful failure in 1948 to help Palestinians defend themselves and return to Palestine. When my father tried to return to Jaffa, he was arrested. For many years he was suspected of not supporting the government and was harassed and imprisoned. I also knew that the regime obstructed any development projects that might have benefited Palestinians on the West Bank. It concentrated on the East Bank and favoured the Jordanians at the expense of Palestinian citizens. I grew up feeling only hostility towards the Jordanian regime. I remember an argument I had as a ten-year-old with friends. I was considering joining the Boy Scouts and was told I would have to pledge allegiance to the Jordanian monarch. I couldn't do this. Even when I didn't know what it meant to be Palestinian, I knew I was not Jordanian.

Meanwhile, the Israeli army was forging a national identity for its youth. I wished we had an army that could take the burden of having to create my own identity off my hands. How comforting it would be to have an institution like the military to mould our self-image and national identity.

I had no notion that similar feelings had driven many of my compatriots to leave the Occupied Territories and join the fedayeen, or freedom fighters, of Fatah and other Palestinian Liberation Organisation (PLO) factions, transforming themselves into 'new Palestinians' in order to fight Israel with their keffiyehs and Kalashnikovs.

These new Palestinians were responding to years of deprivation. In UN refugee camps in neighbouring Arab countries they had been turned into passive human beings dependent on charity, living under the surveillance of their Arab 'hosts' while they waited for their interminable suffering to end. The image of the new Palestinian was liberating, energising. People like my father also felt they were waking from a deep-seated lethargy as they worked on establishing a Palestinian state in the Gaza Strip, the West Bank and East Jerusalem. But he didn't believe in armed resistance. He was convinced that peace lay in recognising Israel with a Palestinian state beside it.

Perhaps what enabled him to think in these nonconformist ways was that he had enough confidence in himself as a Palestinian. He didn't need to prove anything. He didn't want to be trapped in the past, or draw a line and wipe it clean. He wanted Israel to recognise the Nakba and the Palestinians' historic rights, but he knew there was no return to an earlier way of life. That was over. He was more interested in shaping the future – not through violent means, but through diplomacy. He knew that Jordan would do everything it could to stop him and others who supported

Palestinian statehood, and he paid the price for his politics. His Jordanian passport was withdrawn and he was disbarred. But none of this would deter him and he forged ahead regardless, using every opportunity to advocate his vision.

My father seemed miles ahead of everyone else. He was a brilliant, daring lawyer who never hesitated to do what he believed in. In 1949 he travelled with others to Lausanne to negotiate with Israel for the return of the refugees. In 1953 he won a case against Barclays Bank that allowed Palestinian refugees access to the accounts Israel had seized from them, resulting in the return of substantial sums of money to the holders of these accounts. He always thought of novel ways to do what he felt was possible. And despite the fact that Israel's rise had caused him so much suffering, somehow he could not hate those who had occasioned all this pain. He didn't know how to be vengeful. He genuinely believed in the good that could come to the Middle East from the cooperation between these two peoples.

But Israel, which was now behaving with imperial arrogance, was not interested in peace with the Palestinians. This might have been why Israel's foreign minister, Moshe Dayan, wanted to invite figures known for their opposition to Sadat's initiative, such as the mayors of Nablus, Ramallah and Hebron, to Sadat's welcome reception at Tel Aviv airport. All of them refused. Dayan also instructed Menahem Milson, Sadat's aide-de-camp during his visit to Jerusalem, not to include my father on the invitation list.

This would free Israel from having to negotiate with the Palestinians.

I was more inclined to follow my father's vision than the PLO's. Those images of Palestinians with guns, all the iconic posters, songs, poetry and romanticism, left me cold.

Like my father, I was impressed with what I saw of Israel. Unlike the provincialism of Jordan, Israelis seemed open to the world. The spirit of philanthropy was alive and well there, with so many initiatives funded by rich Jews from all over the world. It looked as though people's worth was not measured by their material possessions. Most people rode well-maintained buses and only a few people had fancy cars. They lived in simple flats and did not see the need to build palaces as our well-to-do people did. High officials and politicians were addressed by their first name – so different from Jordan, with its elaborate titles. In correspondence they did not address their officials with 'your highness' or 'your excellency'; they just wrote the initials 'a' and 'd', Hebrew for 'respected sir'. They did not wear ties or jackets. Even in their parliament, they wore open collars. They had a good welfare system, free education all the way through university, free health care and a pension system that meant that the family's well-being did not rely on their children. All this enabled more social mobility. It reduced children's dependence on their parents and allowed them to pursue their own lives. There was even the possibility, which appealed to me, of choosing a new name, a new place to live, a new community. It would be like being reborn, recreating yourself anew, being master of your own fate.

I had tried to minimise my expenses during my studies in London so I would not be beholden to my father. Yet regardless of all my attempts to break free from my family, my life could never be completely independent of them. I yearned to have a life of my own, which for young Israeli men of my age seemed entirely possible. They also had democracy and freedom of expression. I could not read their Hebrew newspapers but was impressed by how freely the English-language *Jerusalem Post* published opinions critical of the government. I contributed poems and articles to the youth page. For that I was taken aside by the president of Birzeit College, where I was studying, and told in no uncertain terms that it was wrong to contribute to a Zionist newspaper.

In Israel it appeared possible to criticise the highest officials. They could be tried in court if they committed an offence. The courts seemed to be independent and to provide a safeguard against corruption. They also had a law that every letter written to an official must be answered. If the sender did not like the answer, there was always an appeal process, so you never felt like you were at the mercy of lazy or corrupt officials who could simply disregard you. It was all so unlike the way officialdom and politics operated in Jordan. Unlike the staid, oppressed people around us, Israelis came across as active, adventurous and confident. Nothing seemed to stand in their way. They had a deep appreciation of Western classical music and an excellent music radio

station, which I listened to, as well as superb live concerts and a music academy that produced world-class
musicians. They were creative and organised. Why not
learn from them? Why not put the nineteen years of
backward Jordanian rule behind us – nineteen years of
stagnation while Israel moved ahead and built a new
society? And for a young man like me, nineteen years
was a long time.

I was also highly impressed by the socialist kibbutz
experiment. Later on I wondered whether my interest
in living in an ashram in Pondicherry, India, in the
early 1970s might have been my way of experiencing
what the early Zionists had tried to do – experiment-
ing in new ways of living and getting away from the
shackles of family and traditional society.

Perhaps, I thought, the Israelis would be more
likely to understand me and my search for an alternative society than traditional Palestinians, who seemed
intolerant of change and difference, and could not
begin to accept that I had chosen to leave London for
India to try my hand at a spiritual life.

This matter of national character was on my mind.
It was what I discussed with Henry during that first
encounter. When I spoke of my admiration for how
I thought Israel was forging a national personality,
Henry looked sceptical. He said he did not see it like
that. Being a pacifist, he did not like the emphasis on
the military. He was influenced by the views of people
like Ahad Ha'am, the founder of cultural Zionism, who
favoured a secular vision of Israel as a Jewish spiritual
centre, not necessarily a state for Jews.

Henry

Henry had just arrived in Israel from Cyprus after finishing his doctorate in psychology at Yale University. He had no idea whether he would be staying in Israel and, if he did, what he would do. Or at least he didn't tell me. In Cyprus he had witnessed the terrible effects of the partition of the small island between the ethnic Turkish community and the ethnic Greek community, with the expulsion of the Greek Cypriots from the Turkish part of the island. He had made it a point to visit both Greek and Turkish sectors and felt for the refugees and the injustice they were suffering.

Of the little he knew about Israel and Palestine, he suspected that a similar situation existed there. As he made his way to Israel, he felt certain that he would be unable to keep silent about what was happening. He would most likely get arrested once he became involved in political activities. What form that would take and what would be the nature of his involvement he did not know.

I noticed that Henry was drinking his coffee black and asked why.

'I'm lactose-intolerant,' he said.

'So am I.'

'Seventy per cent of Semites are. We both belong to the same racial group and are among the majority of intolerants,' he said, laughing heartily.

In the hotel foyer, there was a lot of smoking, which bothered Henry. He was a non-smoker (his mother's death was smoking-related, so he couldn't stand it) and he did not drink. We went outside on to a balcony to get some fresh air.

As we stood there, Henry told me that he was a vegetarian and that he observed the Sabbath. Explaining how this had come about, he told me that he had gone to Madagascar to study burial rituals after the death of his mother. She had died very suddenly. He and his siblings had tried their best but failed to resuscitate her. Ever since, he had been fascinated by death rituals. Whenever he found a dead animal on the road he stopped to give it a burial.

'Even on the highway?' I asked

'Yes. I cannot tolerate seeing a creature left unburied.'

Then he told me about his 'death, decay and resurrection.' It was a fascinating tale.

'I don't remember everything from my time in Madagascar,' he said, 'but I recall drinking salt water as an emetic. I have always suffered from constipation, which was severe at the time. Then vomiting, diarrhoea, passing out on a supply truck coming down from the north of the island. I came close to death and to madness.

'At the time I thought I was Moses. I am coming back, bringing miracles. I am the Creator. I must say the Word to bring about the Light of Day. These are the things I do remember.

'I was rescued by a relative of mine, Dave Allon, who called his Madagascan friend, who then called his relative, a Cabinet minister. The minister sent in an air force jet fighter that flew me from Ile Sainte-Marie, which is also known as the Island of Abraham. I then flew on Air Madagascar to London via Jedda. I was put on an antipsychotic drug by a French neuro-psychia-trist, who told my sister, Ilana, "If he is nervous, give him more." The effect of the overdose was my jaw was dislocated, my arms were wheeling, my legs bicycling out of control. At the time, I was terrified I was crazy. The medicine was driving a wedge between me and my body. I thought, "So that is how it is: I will be like a mad traveller within my own body."'

I tried my best to relate to this, but it was not easy. I had once practised yoga at the Sri Aurobindo Ashram in Pondicherry for a few weeks before being called home because my mother fell ill. This brief stay had helped me come to a better understanding of the split between the body and the mind. But it was surely nothing like what Henry had experienced.

He continued, 'In London, Ilana turned to me and said, in her most authoritative tone, "Look, you have to pull yourself together for five minutes. Then you can do what you like." I go up to the British immigra-tion officer and say, "My name is Henry Abramovitch and I just had a nervous breakdown." Since I have a stamped medical visa, documents, certificates from a private doctor, he waves me through rather than create a scene.

'My sister later told me that she never thought I would leave the island alive. She also said that I made a vow that if I ever left Madagascar alive, I'd become vegetarian and respect the Shabbat.' Then, in a lower voice, he added, 'In my own way.'

I believed I could find more similarities between Henry's experiences and my own. What was common to both of us was our transformative time in a distant land – in his case remaining in Madagascar, in my case Pondicherry – and delving deeper and deeper into ourselves. We both wanted to write about the experience and were both struggling to do so.

Living in the stifling, traditional society of Ramallah, I have always worked by finding small orchards of time and space of my own. I would escape to the surrounding hills for solitary walks and on Saturdays I would stay away from my father's law office to dedicate the day to writing. But my father would not leave me alone. He always made appointments for me and found things that he said urgently needed to be done that day. I was looking for solace in the midst of the chaos all around, and I found it with Henry.

At that point in my life my primary concern was trying to figure out my life. I was looking for a friend who would share my interests in literature, writing, self-analysis and walking, and who would help me understand the last eight years of my life since I left high school. Henry appeared to be the friend I was looking for. We continued talking on that hotel balcony in Tel Aviv, moving from one subject to another. It was as though I was testing his range of interests. A close rapport developed between us, the beginnings of a satisfying relationship.

'Would you come to visit me in Ramallah?' I asked, and he immediately agreed. I began to plan in my head where to walk with my new friend.

The other Israelis in the foyer listened to the Egyptian leader selectively and felt euphoric, hearing what they liked and ignoring what they were unwilling to consider, like the necessity to create a Palestinian state and recognise the right of return if peace were ever to prevail. There was a sense of relief in the air: here was the leader of the largest Arab state cutting himself off from other Arab states and proposing peace with Israel. This was what they heard him say.

Over the next months, Henry and I took many walks in the hills. We enjoyed our time together tremendously. We began planning other excursions in far-off places where I could not walk alone. We were a striking pair, Henry and I, he with his long, bushy beard and me scampering along beside him like a mountain goat, small, spritely and clean-shaven. Both short, one stocky, the other thin, we would stride down the hills in the Galilee or walk along the pebbly shore of the Dead Sea or through the Ramallah hills. And talking, always talking. We walked and talked endlessly, filling the hills with our chatter and laughter. I told him about my writing. I read to him what I was working on and his advice was helpful.

One day we went to Jaffa looking for the grave of a friend of my family in what had been the Dajani Hospital. Dr Fuad Dajani, the founder of the hospital, had died suddenly and his wife had intended to build him the most beautiful tomb in Palestine, but her plans had been interrupted by the Nakba. The site was now a maternity hospital. In the grounds, as we tried to follow the hand-drawn map his widow had given us indicating the whereabouts of the grave, we were confronted by a security guard. He said there was no Arab grave there and ordered us to leave, erasing with one single sweep of his hand the entire history of the site. It was infuriating. Henry was as incensed as I was. He argued with the guard, insisting that the grave was there. He could not tolerate this denial of a Palestinian presence in Jaffa.

After we had made our retreat, Henry turned to me and said, 'We were looking on the wrong side, you know.' I took out the old woman's map. He was right.

Another time we decided to go to the Dead Sea and sleep overnight on the shore. A car dropped us before the turn-off to Jericho and we set out on foot. I felt a new kind of excitement, striking off the road into unknown territory where you could get lost or arrested because of the area's proximity to the Jordanian border. At that time no restrictions on movement had yet been imposed. For the first time in my life I was off the beaten track, going beyond the lunar hills towards the wall of boulders where the salty sea nestled and into the reeds, all the way down to the water and the lowest point on earth, to sleep in the open and listen to the waves whipping against the smooth rocks. Shortly before dawn, we heard an army jeep driving by and I held my breath until it passed. This was a military area and had the soldiers seen us we would surely have been arrested. Or worse, they could have driven over us as we slept. After the jeep passed, I could no longer sleep. The soldiers had destroyed the peace. I stayed up listening to the wind and the sound of the waves rushing in, then receding, sometimes softly hissing as they washed off the salt that had crystallised on the shore.

In the morning we looked for the nearby kibbutz, where we had breakfast. I was breaking every rule that a Palestinian could break.

On his own Henry did many more crazy things. I worried about him – how he would be viewed by the Palestinians he encountered on the way and whether someone would do him harm. But he welcomed adventure.

Once he went to the Latrun salient north-west of Jerusalem, an area that Israel had annexed immediately after the 1967 war. He went to visit the Trappist monastery there and slept out in the open in a region where such things were not done. As a Palestinian I would be arrested if I were found there carrying my sleeping bag outdoors, but for Henry it was different. The army would just assume he was an eccentric Jew, not a terrorist.

On another occasion he visited Hebron, one of the most dangerous flashpoints in the Occupied Territories. He went on his own and did not ask for contacts before venturing into this new area. When he returned I asked him how it was and he told me he had met some kind Palestinians who invited him to sleep the night at their house. He didn't speak Arabic and they had only rudimentary English, and yet they seemed to have managed to get by. Henry was a great communicator and was able to bring out the best in people. He laughed like a young man, a fulsome rolling laugh that was infectious and never failed to endear him to everyone. He genuinely believed in the brotherhood of all men and was sure that ultimately good would prevail. He was a pacifist, always looking for kindness in people. This is why he was fearless on his hikes. He looked at the people he met with an open, friendly smile, never with fear or bad expectations, and he had a great capacity for empathy. He always found people to befriend and to stay with, whether they were Israelis or Palestinians.

Henry was always trying to find the moral centre in his religion and make it relevant. He invited me to share the Seder meal with him and his friends where he tried to interpret the exodus from Egypt as representative of the passage into freedom of all nations, including the Palestinians. He wholeheartedly wished that the Palestinians would also find freedom.

In 1979 I did something that was unusual for an unmarried Palestinian man living in the same town as his parents: I moved out of my father's house and rented a small one-room flat, where I lived alone. It was an oasis of tranquillity. I could have my friends visit me there. I could listen to the music I liked and write undisturbed. Henry often came to visit. Once I showed him the first chapter of the autobiographical novel I had written. He immediately said he wanted to read it aloud to me.

At the time, my writing was still heavily influenced by other writers and their concerns. I had not yet found my own voice. I had read my scribblings to friends, but they were more concerned with what I wrote rather than the style in which I wrote it, unlike Henry. This was why it was important to have Henry's views. He took the manuscript, stood up, brushed his beard away from his mouth and began to read in his melodious voice. As he did, I could hear the voice that I was searching for.

I was proud of my friendship with Henry. After one of our walks he told me, 'Every time we walk together I understand more about the meaning of friendship.' My friendship with Henry was a profound relationship, more so than any I had been able to forge with a Palestinian.

It was the late 1970s and we were living in a dream. I was young and ambitious, and I believed it would all work out well between Palestinians and Israelis, and that Henry and I would always be friends. I had published my first book on human rights, *The West Bank and the Rule of Law*, which was getting considerable attention and I then believed it could help in curbing the abuses that were occurring, such as the acquisition of Palestinian land for Jewish settlements, the demolition of Palestinian houses, the closure of banks, the collective punishments and restrictions on free speech and assembly. The human rights organisation I helped to establish in 1979, Al-Haq, was making progress, creating a stir and highlighting the human rights violations perpetrated by the Israeli military. But even more significant to me was the work I thought we were doing to entrench the rule of law in our own Palestinian society. One aspect of Israel that I admired was that it had laws its society lived by. This also contributed to its national identity and I wanted the same for us. At the time I also thought Israel would be ultimately accountable to international law, especially if any violations were exposed and if fellow organisations around the world supported our efforts.

We were encouraged to believe this by the replies we received to the interventions we sent to the military legal adviser. Al-Haq's letters, pamphlets and books would invariably receive responses. This meant that we were in constant dialogue with Israeli officials over legal matters. As long as there was dialogue, there was hope. If we reached an impasse with a legal adviser, we could always resort to the Israeli High Court.

I was hopeful that a political solution could be found and life would improve. I was hopeful that reason and kindness would prevail and the Left in Israel would succeed in bringing an end to the occupation. I was hopeful that, through an association with Israel, we could now modernise quickly.

Henry shared my hopes.

In January 1980 the peace treaty between Egypt and Israel negotiated at Camp David came into effect. Contrary to what Sadat had promised, Israel's withdrawal from the Palestinian territory occupied since 1967 was not a condition of his country's recognition of Israel, which withdrew only from the Sinai Peninsula. Meanwhile, the Likud government under Israel's sixth prime minister, Menachem Begin, was speeding up the establishment of Jewish settlements. Over a hundred were established in our midst.

There was a time in the early days of the occupation

when I had tried to relate to Israel and Israelis as if there was no occupation. That time was over. The occupation was turning into a colonial regime that deprived us of our land and gave our natural resources, our land and water, to their own people. In every way, large and small, it affected our lives and restricted our prospects. To fight this we Palestinians were left to fend for ourselves.

Inevitably, politics began to cast a dark shadow over my relationship with Henry. Unlike Henry, I did not have the luxury of ignoring politics. Henry might express his objection to what was taking place, but he never had to follow this with any concrete political action. He could go on with his life as if nothing was happening. Meanwhile, we Palestinians were subjected to harsh treatment by the Israeli forces – long curfews, house demolitions, censorship, and restrictions on academic freedom and travel. Most aspects of our life were curtailed in some form or another and subject to permits from the military authorities. The occupation determined my present and my future. I waited in long lines for permits and endured constant harassment by the military on the way to and from my office. Even a task as simple as installing a telephone line was an ordeal requiring a military permit that was difficult to obtain.

The first time I sensed any friction in our relationship was in the late 1970s, when I visited Henry's family home and met his father, who struck me as a very kind man, much like Henry. I went with Henry and his family to a synagogue. It was my first visit to a Jewish place of worship. Henry explained to me the setting and the rituals. I did not know much then about Judaism and was curious to learn.

Henry's father was not religious and did not have a beard. This made me curious about what had made Henry decide to grow his. When I asked him, he said he thought I only asked because I wished he were not a Jew. This surprised me, since this was the last thing on my mind. What I really wished for was that he did not become Israeli. The Israelis were my enemies, not the Jews. Surely he understood this. We didn't discuss the matter further, although I was left wondering whether he could ever forget that I'm Palestinian. I worried that, to him, I was not an individual but a representative of my people and that it gratified him to have an Arab friend – something he could boast about. That made me uncomfortable.

For a while in the early 1980s Henry lived in a flat lent to him by a friend in the Montefiore quarter opposite the Old City wall. It had been built at the end of the nineteenth century on land bought by the Jewish banker Moses Montefiore to house Jews from the Old City and ease overcrowding there. It had since become an upmarket neighbourhood, and with a panoramic view of the Old City walls and its historic windmill, it remains one of my favourite parts of Jerusalem. It was also near the newly built cinema, the Cinematheque, and film archive, the first of its kind in Jerusalem. I often met Henry there and we would walk together in that attractive area, even as terrible events were beginning to take place all around us.

Decades later – after he had become a Jungian analyst and university professor, had published a few books and many scholarly articles – every time I approach the building where Henry used to live I recall that magical time when I was still young and full of enthusiasm and confidence about the future. From this vantage point I used to be able to see where the border had been drawn between East and West Jerusalem before 1967. I could also see Silwan, one of the highly congested Palestinian suburbs in the valley just outside the walls of the Old City.

Now, standing there, I can see not only the beautiful walls of the Old City but another wall, ugly and concrete, that looms on the horizon, demarcating a new separation causing further hardship for non-Jewish residents. I can still see Silwan, which is now under vicious attack by the right-wing settler organisation Ateret Cohanim, which is trying to evict the Palestinians, take over their homes and revive what they claim was the City of David.

From our very first meeting at the hotel in Tel Aviv, Henry always maintained that it was tradition that had attracted him to Israel. 'I came not intending to stay,' he told me, 'and then things happened.' But can you live in Israel and not take responsibility for what its government is doing to non-Jews living there?

I have often asked myself what I should expect of a friend. I tried to disassociate Henry from what he was not directly responsible for. Yet with the ongoing theft of our land, restrictions on our daily lives and the establishment of Jewish settlements, this was difficult, at times impossible. In the early 1980s, through Al-Haq and its field workers in the Occupied Territories, I learned more of what was taking place around me. I became less involved in my own story and began to write about other people. The more I knew, the angrier I became. I did not feel Henry shared my concern about the large-scale violation of human rights and the dismal future that awaited us Palestinians living in the Occupied Territories and we began to drift apart.

3

Visiting Jaffa

Jaffa, 1978

I don't know why I was obsessed with spending a night in Jaffa, my father's city, from which he was exiled. Daytime visits, like mine with Henry, were somehow not enough; I had to spend the night there. I had heard so much about it and thought that I needed at least one night to give me a true taste of what it was like to live in the city of my youthful imaginings. Perhaps I wanted to experience a return of sorts. Perhaps I wanted to understand what it was like for my father to live in a coastal city rather than in landlocked Ramallah. But, with the Israeli occupation, it was rare for me to spend a night away from home, and it was only in the autumn of 1978 that I was able to do this, when I visited a Jewish lawyer colleague, David, and his wife, Sarah.

When I was growing up in what was then the village of Ramallah, I would stand at the foot of the brown hills near our house and look at the sliver of blue sea that was visible on the horizon on a clear day.

At the time the sea was inaccessible because of the border with Israel, but after the 1967 war, the lifting of the border between Israel and the West Bank allowed us to venture from the central hills of the West Bank all the way to the sea.

When we used to drive from Ramallah to Jaffa, we could see the transformation Israel had wrought on the land. Just before we got to Jaffa my father would point to the side of the road at where in the distance the Arab towns of Abasieh, Beit Dajan, Yazour and Salameh had once stood. I could never see any remains, but in one place there was still an old tree – I believe it was a carob – whose dusty branches had probably shaded the road to Jaffa when my father had lived there. My first impression of Jaffa as we entered was of a crumbling city with a fading charm but disgraced by neglect, as any city can be. My father said it was unchanged, as though time had stood still. Except for the Manshieh quarter, which had been completely destroyed, the city was more or less intact. Ever the optimist, he had thought that it would become part of the new Arab state under the UN partition scheme of 1947.

Usually the conqueror tries as quickly as possible to repair the damage caused by the war and have life return to normal. This is how it was with Jerusalem, Ramallah and other cities in the West Bank and Gaza after Israel conquered them in 1967. Not so with Jaffa after the 1948 war. The inhabitants were not allowed to return and those 2,500 or so Palestinians who managed to stay were forced out of their homes and placed in the Ajami quarter of the city. Surrounded by barbed wire, it was like a ghetto, and permission from the military governor was needed to enter and exit the zone. As for the rest of the city, the victorious Israelis were at a loss. Ideas ranged from total destruction to the renovation of the existing houses. Many of the small stone-built villages in the Galilee, which the Israeli army destroyed in 1948 and 1949, were relatively easy to demolish. In their place, they planted trees. Razing a historic 5,000-year-old city like Jaffa was not so easy.

May 1948 was not the first time that Jaffa had been evacuated. Although the city had prospered during the Second World War, it had been a war zone during the First World War. My grandmother Mary, my father's stepmother, remembered how her family had been forced to leave Jaffa by the Ottomans. After the war was over, the inhabitants were allowed back, but it was unlikely that a similar return would be possible after 1948.

Some Israeli families were moved into the city but many houses stood empty. Sarah, an artist whose family came from Poland, was one of the few who took matters into their own hands, convincing her reluctant husband to move their family from Tel Aviv to one of these empty Jaffa homes. She thought they were charming and had character. To me, Jaffa was a conquered city.

I entered the house with a heavy heart. It was an old Arab house with a porch and small garden. It was divided by an unattractive concrete wall into two dwellings and seemed shabby and in need of renovation.

All sorts of complicated thoughts rushed through my head. Strangely I felt neither anger nor reproach. I just wanted to understand how it had all been possible: the Nakba, the expulsion of the city's inhabitants, the new inhabitants in the homes of the conquered.

What would become of the city and of us?

My first visit to Jaffa had been right after the beginning of the occupation of the West Bank, when I was sixteen. I drove with my parents to visit the city they had been forced to leave nineteen years earlier.

We went first to my mother's family house on Nuzha Street and met the Romanian family who had moved in. The encounter was more surreal than sad. The portly woman wearing a long dark dress who opened the door had no idea who we were. She looked confused and scared at the sight of us. Perhaps she had never been told that she had been given the house of a Palestinian family. We had no language in common and she could not understand a word we said. She was baffled when we made our way inside and my mother began to explain the function of every room in the house. My father seemed embarrassed by the whole experience. He could not wait to leave. My mother, on the other hand, moved through the house as though she owned it, pointing out the beautiful floor tiles, which she emphasised to us were Portland stone of the best quality. 'Look how after all these years they still shine. My father always wanted to have the best material.' They seemed to be the only remaining feature of the house that was familiar to her. It saddened her that she had to ask permission to enter her own house.

My parents began bickering. My father wanted us to leave immediately, while my mother insisted that he was always in a hurry and we must see every room in the house. For my part, I tried to imagine the house as they had described it – with the stylish furniture and the delicate carved room dividers, or paravans, and the wall hangings. I tried to recall the various family photographs I had seen which showed some of the expensive rugs and the beautiful porcelain figurines the family owned. My parents looked so happy in these photographs. Now they looked wretched, with clenched, grim faces, as they were confronted by denuded walls and alienating surroundings. After we left the house, my father's driving, already bad, was worse than ever.

I had grown up hearing stories about Jaffa, and the more we saw of the city now the more I thought it had been insulted by sheer neglect. The faded beauty of its narrow streets and palatial homes along al-Ajami was marred by the scurrying rats and the broken doors and windows. I found the discrepancy between how the city appeared to my parents and how I saw it disconcerting. I wanted to show my appreciation but I couldn't. I tried hard to see the grandeur of Nuzha Street, about which I had heard so much, but to me it looked shabby, its gardens filled with dying plants.

Jaffa was not just another city in Palestine; it had been the rich, thriving cultural capital of Palestine. It was where everything had happened. So many cities around the world had seen greater devastation during the Second World War than Jaffa had endured in 1948, but those cities were rebuilt soon after the war – Berlin, Nagasaki, Dresden. Not so Jaffa.

I had no doubt my father still saw in his mind's eye the vital city Jaffa used to be. When we visited, he showed me where the cafés, cinemas and houses of his friends used to be – all now gone. Without difficulty, he drove to the outskirts of the city where, near the sea, he showed us some empty land he had bought just before the Nakba. He had been planning to build a new house for himself, his wife and daughter there. It was not to be. My father left us inside the car, saying he would not be long, and went to walk on the land. When he came back he was in a sombre mood. He said nothing. He wasn't one to give easy expression to his emotions. Nor was it his habit to complain. I was left to wonder how my life would have been had I been raised in that house by the sea rather than in the hills of Ramallah.

I was not alone in my desire to return to the city. Many others were making their own way back to Jaffa, among them two men of my father's generation, Mousa and Halim, who related to Jaffa in very different ways.

Mousa was one of a small minority in the West Bank who were not unhappy with the occupation. For them it provided new business opportunities and the chance to once again visit the city of their birth, the city they loved. Many like him made their peace with Israel, glad to be rid of Jordanian rule with its thinly veiled prejudice against Palestinians.

Originally from a humble background, Mousa was a labour contractor for some Israeli construction firms.

He recruited Palestinian workers for them to work on projects in Israel and in the settlements. It was a lucrative business and he was quickly becoming a rich man. His friends began calling him Moshe.

For nineteen years after the Nakba, he had missed Jaffa. Under the occupation, he could now go back as an affluent man and eat like a lord at the seafront fish restaurants there. Mousa began to act as though nothing bad had happened – no Nakba and no occupation. He did not care that Israel was preventing refugees from returning to Jaffa. He had accomplished his own victorious return and his motto was now 'Forget, forgive and live'. On weekends he drove his car along the Latrun road from the West Bank and was able to reach the sea he loved in forty-five minutes. Once in Jaffa, he would walk around the city, his belly protruding in front of him, his arms dangling by his side, palms turned backwards as he pressed forward, light on his feet despite his bulk – he was a good dancer.

He was on excellent terms with the officials working for the military government, in particular one Arabic-speaking Israeli who doubled as an intelligence agent. The agent enjoyed mingling with Arabs and had settled his family in one of the Arab quarters of East Jerusalem, where a lifelong friendship developed between the two men. Mousa met him frequently, providing him with information when needed and arranging for him to meet people he needed to investigate. He allowed the agent to use his house to hide the money he had illegally acquired from bribes. In return, Mousa obtained commissions and all sorts of permits to make his life as comfortable as possible. Both men agreed that life was good. It was only marred by those Palestinian rebels – Israel called *mukhar-ibeen* – who planted bombs and complicated relations between the two sides. They should have realised there was no point fighting Israel.

People like Mousa began to contact friends and family who had stayed in Israel after 1948. Palestinian families from across the old divide began to intermarry. But Israel became concerned that these emerging alliances would bring this split society back together again. They wanted a greater Israel for the Jews, not a united Palestine for the Arabs, and from this concern grew ideas of once again separating the two areas. This was not accomplished until more than fifteen years later, by which time Mousa had gone into retirement as a rich man.

Halim's case was different. His return from London to Jaffa, the city of his birth, had to wait until after the Oslo Accord in 1995, the result of secret negotiations in Oslo between Israel and the PLO. It had promised real peace and instead delivered a mere repackaging of the occupation. But one of the few concessions Israel made was that it allowed a number of Palestinian members of the PLO to return to the Occupied Territories. Halim was a businessman who had joined the PLO in 1973. Tall and well built, he was slightly stooped, with large piercing black eyes and bushy eyebrows. He was active as a public speaker for the Palestinian cause. After his return, he settled in Ramallah and became a frequent visitor to Jaffa.

When I first met Halim I disliked him. Why was he here? He had come too late, after the disastrous Oslo Accords, which had so compromised Palestinian rights. What Palestine did he think he was returning to? Where was he when we could still have ended the occupation, when there had still been a chance to build on what we had? He was too busy pursuing his own interests. Now he had returned on a tourist visa, using his British passport, while the PLO, which he had served for so many years, had surrendered.

After each visit to Jaffa he would come back and with great enthusiasm describe to me how unchanged he found the city to be. He had that uncanny capacity to ignore everything that had happened to the residents of the city who stayed, as though their lives were of no importance, as though they were dispensable and all that was important was the bricks and mortar of the city itself. History was measured by his own experience. It ended when he left and resumed when he returned. Whatever happened in the interim was of no significance. 'Just imagine,' he told me with even greater excitement than usual, 'the young Palestinian boys playing in the street knew all the Arabic names of the streets. They could give me directions as if nothing had changed. It's the same Jaffa I knew as a young man.' I wondered what the people in Jaffa thought of him – the Arab who left, now returned.

After Oslo, I was miserable. Could he understand what I felt? When I tried to tell him, he would stop me and begin describing loudly and emphatically his most recent visit to Jaffa and how he'd been for a swim in

the sea just as he used to do as a young man. He made
much of the few iconic businesses that still survived
from his time in the city back then: the Fakhri Jday
pharmacy, the Abulafia bakery and the now famous
hummus place, Abu Hasan's. From these, he recon-
structed the entire city. There was a desperation about
his selective memory.

I will never forget his description of his first visit to
Jaffa after his return. It was like a fleeting realisation
that others had stayed and suffered and that the city is
not just the bricks and mortar. But he soon forgot all
this. It was the stark contradiction between these two
states of mind that could exist in him side by side that
stood out and made me remember his description of
this experience:

> In the middle of all the dereliction, I saw a small
> house on top of Rabieh, the hill that overlooks
> the sea. Next to it was a jasmine tree, in bloom,
> which caught my eye, and I swear it was the
> same jasmine tree from when I was a young
> man. I decided to walk up to the house and knock
> on the door. As I approached, I noticed the tree's
> stems close to the ground. They looked ancient,
> but they seemed to sustain the growth of the
> delicate branches higher up. These were covered
> with white flowers like a small constellation of
> stars.
>
> Except for that house with the blossoming
> jasmine tree, the sense of desolation in the
> city troubled me. I went in search of things I

remembered from when I was young, trying to reconstruct the city from memory. I found many reminders of that time. The roads formed the same grid as I remember. Very few new roads had been added. Many of the old buildings were still standing, but they were in a bad state. Some buildings had been demolished.

I was fifteen when we left. I was preparing for my final exams. Leaving was so painful to me that I decided to put the city out of my mind, to look forward, not back. I went to work in Saudi Arabia at a time when the offices still didn't have air conditioning. I worked hard in difficult conditions. I had to tolerate being described as a refugee, a man without a country, like some sort of bastard. But I never allowed myself to feel self-pity. I told myself: the world is my country. First I was a Saudi citizen, then a British citizen. That opened up many lucrative financial opportunities and I made the most of them. I became a millionaire and bought a summer house in Monaco, another in Paris and a third in the mountains of Lebanon. I lived well and forgot all about the city of my youth until I retired. It was then that the memories began to come back. Then I had a strong urge to visit the city and find out what had become of it.

It was not an easy decision. It took courage. I knew that it would bring back all sorts of memories. Just the sight of my family's house would open old wounds. To prepare myself I

tried to imagine myself standing in front of
our old veranda with its white tiles edged in
black. After leaving Jaffa, I had abandoned so
much. I had brought to an end one way of life,
a life with a family in a closely knit community
with a predictable future. Instead, I pursued a
more solitary life. In Jeddah, I lived alone until
I married one of the foreign secretaries at the
company where I was working. I had very little
contact with the rest of my family, especially
after the death of my parents. I had a certain
freedom. I was the master of my own life. But
now that I was back in Jaffa, walking up the
familiar streets, I felt as though I was back in the
grid I had extricated myself from. I realised how
much I'd missed my old self.

As I saw more of the town, I began to be
obsessed by a single question: why did we leave?
The few bombs that had been thrown at the
Manshieh quarter seemed like nothing compared
to what Beirut had experienced in 1982. The
Lebanese had not abandoned their city en masse.
Why had we? Why did we leave everything and
just go? What sort of people were we to have
taken off, leaving everything behind?

The particulars of that moment began to
come back: how my father, always a stubborn
man, refused to go and my mother pleaded with
him to leave. My father then fell silent. In their
exile he and my mother became estranged, as
though he blamed her for tricking him into

leaving. This was harder for me than anything I had gone through until then. I lost not only Jaffa but my parents as well.

In retrospect I wonder what it would have been like if we had stayed. It was true that my parents were older and might not have been able to endure the hardship of staying. But I could have. Why didn't I insist on remaining in our house and taking care of our property? What could the Israelis have done to me? Impose a curfew? Restrict my movements? I've experienced all this, and worse, in the war in Lebanon – for three months I was trapped in Beirut and couldn't leave. If I had stayed in Jaffa I might not have been able to afford expensive houses around the world, but the whole world would have meant little to me if I'd had my Jaffa.

I went to Rabieh, the highest place in the city, and looked out to sea. No other sea was as beautiful or as blue. The memories began to flood back. I could almost see myself, still slim and muscular, in my bathing trunks, swimming far out into the sea.

I had to rest. I was feeling out of breath. I found a low wall and leaned against it. Across the wall I saw the cemetery where so many of my father's friends who had died before 1948 were buried. My whole life seemed a waste. I concentrated on the sea and tried to follow the movements of my young self from our house down the hill into the sea. In every place I've been, what I had was what I could afford to buy. I looked for the best and bought it. But this place has a meaning to me that no amount of money could buy. All the money I had amassed could not buy me the feeling of being home. This was the home that I would never be able to replace with any other.

When I walked up to the door of that house I did not know what to expect. It was just a whim. I remembered that the Khaders and their two daughters had lived here. I used to like walking by this house after school in the hope that I would see them standing there in the garden. The house looked inhabited and I was curious to find out who was now living in it.

I knocked. Leila, one of the two daughters, opened the door. Her sister, Nadia, appeared at her side. They had always been on the plump side but now they were practically round. I introduced myself. When they heard my name they jumped with joy and asked me in.

As I sat in their living room with the handsome floor-length window and had a view of the sea, I could hardly believe I was there. Their house had the aura of an old Jaffa house. It was as though nothing had changed.

'Lemonade?' they asked me. They seemed to speak in unison.

Leila disappeared and returned with a tall glass of freshly squeezed lemonade, made from the lemons growing on a tree in their backyard. She had added a few leaves of mint. A white crocheted napkin was carefully folded underneath the glass.

They asked me about my life. I told them. As I spoke I was aware that I was speaking about exile to those who had refused to be exiled. All the time I continued to think how fortunate they were. I both admired and envied them. How trite and empty my life must seem to them. They had never left their beautiful house on Rabieh, overlooking the sea. All the time I spoke they listened to me with unwavering interest.

I asked them about their life.

Leila said, and there was sadness in her voice, 'As you can see, we never left. Mother was ill at the time and we did not want to disturb her. Father thought nothing could be worse for us than to leave our house. If need be we would die here. We lost both our parents in 1960 and ever since we have been living on our own. Not a day passes when we don't ask each other, why didn't we leave? Most of the people who left have done so well for themselves. We stayed here alone, in a dead and empty city. There used to be 70,000 people living here, now there are only around 2,500 of the original Jaffa people. None of our friends stayed. As you see, we are still single. We have no friends. We have kept our house, but we have also lost our community, our life.'

Hearing this account made me think how often

Palestinians living abroad failed to appreciate what life was like for us who continued to live under Israeli rule, whether in the State of Israel or in the Occupied Territories. It is true that we were spared exile, but it took so much effort to hold on to our identity as Palestinians, to forge a life under regimes that tried to drive us out.

When I went to spend that night in Jaffa I was conscious that, unlike my parents, I came unburdened by memories of Jaffa before the Nakba. But I tried to imagine that life from everything I had heard and read. My first visit to the city was with them, so I was attentive to their feelings and attitudes. This time I had come on my own to explore my reactions to the place I had heard so much about.

My first reaction, though, was simply to sweat. The place was just too humid for me. I'm used to the dry weather of Ramallah.

David and Sarah were hospitable and offered me dinner as soon as I arrived. Sarah put out some bread and some hummus (she pronounced it 'khumus'), over which she had poured a strange-coloured oil. I wondered whether it was actually olive oil but did not want to embarrass her by asking. Unlike an Arab hostess, Sarah did not fuss over her guests. I found this refreshing. We sat in a relaxed way on cushions around a low table, chatting, eating and sipping red wine. I felt good in this house. I still couldn't help wondering what sort of life had been lived here by its former Palestinian owners, but I did not want to follow that train of thought. I was aware that by choosing to sleep here for the night I was a bit player in this tragedy of dispossession. But I reasoned with myself that I was here to cure myself of the longing I felt for Jaffa, which I had inherited from my parents and grandparents.

We talked about what it was like to live in the Occupied Territories. I was curious to know more about Sarah as an artist and asked her about herself. There was much that she wanted to tell me. Her husband, who must have heard it all before, went to bed, leaving us alone.

Sarah told me about her parents' escape from Poland. They had found refuge in Israel but remained Poles to their dying day; their Hebrew was basic. Sarah wondered about the Poland of her parents. Her parents had never spoken about it, and much of their past remained mysterious. They were wrenched out of one life and thrown into another – in the country in which she was born, the only country she knew, the country where she still felt foreign. Perhaps this feeling of foreignness came from her parents' inability to adjust to the ways of the new country. Or perhaps this was the lot of artists and writers.

She had felt more at one with Israeli society before the war of 1967, when there was much to do. She felt she was part of a common struggle for survival and she had no recollection of feeling different from everyone else then. She still felt that way when the time came for her to do her military service. She tried her best to participate and submerge herself in the collective self of the group, but it was with disastrous results. Just three months after being drafted, she was discharged having been deemed unfit for military service. The military psychologist who signed her discharge order prescribed a long period of rest. Nevertheless, Sarah did not feel alienated from those around her. That would come later, after 1967.

The anguish Sarah experienced in the months leading to the war ended with Israel's victory. Now she was sure it was time for peace. What use was winning the war if Israel would not use its power to make peace? But that was not how people around her felt. Victory seemed only to cloud their minds, unleashing a wave of hysterical nationalism, and it caused Sarah to break with her immediate social circle and go in search of new friends. These were leftists whom she, in turn, then alienated by moving to Jaffa.

As she talked I looked around the room. The organisation of space in the house was unconventional. It was so unlike our house in Ramallah, where our living quarters are distinct from the room where we welcome guests. That room has our best furniture and our best ceramic pieces. This house in Jaffa had an improvised feel to it that was nothing like our guest room, with its large sofas. The furniture here had a temporary look as if it had just come from the flea market, where much of the property stolen from Arab homes ended up. Each sofa was different, there was no uniformity, as there would have been in a middle-class Arab home. There was a low table and we reclined on variously coloured cushions around it. It wasn't cosy. There was something unfinished about it, just like Sarah. But I liked the freedom from convention.

Sarah told me, 'When I first moved to Jaffa, many of my friends were deeply disappointed. They could not understand how a lefty like me could move into an Arab house. I can't explain it. I just felt a strong attraction to the old city. What is this self-righteousness, this condemnation? I don't understand it. These very same people teach at Tel Aviv University, which is built over the ruins of an Arab village. Why is that all right but it's not all right to live in a beautiful old Arab house?'

'Then you must understand how Palestinian refugees like my own family feel. They yearn to return to their homes,' I said.

Sarah's tone changed abruptly. 'Listen,' she said, 'in the Second World War there were so many displaced communities. So many borders changed, so many people were uprooted. Europe is brimming with displaced communities. But wherever they ended up, they all picked up and continued with their lives. They didn't languish in refugee camps living off aid like the Palestinians, living in shacks, for God's sake, dependent on handouts. What is this holding on to the past? It's despicable. Why don't you get on with your life? It's pathetic. Look at us, how well we've managed. To survive on charity, for God's sake, for three decades.'

'You mean UNRWA food rations.'

'Yes,' she said, raising her voice. 'Yes, UNRWA.'

'I have my issues with this organisation too, but I

suspect for different reasons from yours,' I said, but Sarah didn't ask me to explain.

I was shocked to hear what she had to say and how she failed to appreciate that for us Palestinians it was not only a question of material losses but the denial of our very existence as a nation. But I decided not to challenge her. I had come to listen, not to argue. I listened without anger or rancour. I just wanted to understand. I was, after all, a guest in her house. I didn't want a confrontation.

She cannot have noticed how her words struck me, for she went on, 'I'm an artist. There is nothing else that I can do in my life. This used to worry my parents, who wanted me to pursue what they called a proper career. I cannot say their nagging hasn't rubbed off. It left me feeling anxious. It's worse during the long days when I'm alone in my studio after David leaves. All alone with only my cat, trying to give abstract expression to my thoughts and feelings. It's a lonely business being an artist. How can one ever be sure whether all the hours spent pursuing intractable thoughts and emotions are well spent ? It's impossible. When it gets bad and I feel I've tied myself in knots I take off, leave the studio and my house and go out. Everyone I meet in the street has something to do. They're all involved in something, the baker in his bakery (what a wonderful thing to be pro-ducing bread – hot, fragrant, round pittas), the carpenter, the blacksmith. None of them wastes time in reflection over what they're doing. They just do it. As for me, the world would go on spinning whether or not I produced my art. What, then, is my work worth? What is it for?'

'What are you working on now?' I asked.

'An installation.'

I had never heard this word before in relation to art.

'I hang things together to represent an idea. I'm not sure yet where it's going. I can show it to you tomorrow and you can tell me what you think. Now, let me show you your room. But first let's clear up.'

When I got up the next morning, David had already left. Sarah was in the kitchen. The cat had climbed into the kitchen sink and was prowling around the crockery, sniffing the leftover hummus. My mother would never have tolerated this. Sarah asked me if I wanted to eat breakfast at Abu Hasan's, 'which makes good khumus'. I was relieved not to have to eat from pots the cat had walked over and so we strolled out together through the old streets of Jaffa. It was late autumn and the air was very humid.

Sarah cut a strange figure here. She wore a grey drop-waist flannel dress with large, low green-coloured pockets. On her feet were brick-coloured moccasins, which came up to her ankles and were fastened with string. She had tied a lock of her auburn hair on top of her head, while the rest of it dangled at the sides like dog's ears. She was tall and lanky, and as she pulled herself up the hill ahead of me I looked at the way she held herself. She did not move gracefully. She walked as though the rest of her body was following her head. First her neck went forward, then came the shoulders, then the swinging arms and finally the feet, which seemed to drag behind. I was curious how the Palestinians we met saw her.

'These are the streets I walk through every time I reach an impasse in my work,' she told me. 'They're always full of Arab children playing in the filth because they have nowhere else to play. Sometimes I stop and talk to them. Hasna, she's a teenager who lives in that house over there. She has become a friend and I often sit with her on her parents' porch and hear about her life. Such a beautiful girl and yet what a dark future she has ahead of her. I would like to help her but I don't know how. He parents are poor. Her brother has taken to trafficking drugs. The poor girl doesn't have much of a future.'

I looked at the names of the streets. They had been struck out and replaced by numbers. Where was Bistress-Iskandar Awad or Jamal Basha or Nuzha Street? Gone, all gone.

Through Hasna, Sarah got to know other Arab girls. Slowly she was coming to understand their problems, not only with their families but also with the municipal and state authorities. Throughout her neighbourhood, the Arab families received no grants and no services. Every attempt was made to make their life so unbearable that they would leave.

'It's my dream to buy one of these old Arab houses before it's demolished,' Sarah said, pointing out where a beautiful Arab house had once stood but had now been reduced to rubble.

When we entered Abu Hasan's, the restaurant was

full of Israelis who, Sarah whispered to me, were left-ists. They flattered themselves into thinking that by coming to eat hummus here they were getting close to the Arabs. They were tourists too.

After breakfast we continued walking along the narrow winding streets. Many of the old Arab houses were still standing, waiting, untouched except by the corrosive salty wind, which pockmarked the walls and rusted the ironwork. As we climbed further up, Sarah stopped before one palatial house and announced that we should go in. The door was open and we just walked through.

Sarah explained, 'You see how these houses are built facing the sea. The plan was very sensible. It allows the wind to pass through the entire house to keep it cool. It's not like the houses in Tel Aviv, which are built with their backs to the sea by people from the interior. Look at the round window up on the wall that faces the sea. You see, there's another window at the same height, also round, on the opposite wall. It was designed to help the air circulate in the house. And look at that delicate cornice all around the top there. How elegant and tasteful. It's my dream to buy one of these houses, renovate it and live in it.'

'Why live in such a theatre of war now?' I asked Sarah.

'I'm an artist,' she said. 'I like beautiful homes.'

We continued our tour. She pointed out small details to me: the iron grille over a row of windows, some beautiful tiles, coloured glass that had survived unbroken. I tried to fill in more details from the photographs I had seen of the various Jaffa families who were friends of my parents – Albina and his parents' wedding, the Dajanis and the life they had lived in the city. All gone now, all in the past. As we passed the empty houses I thought about how their inhabitants had left them fully furnished as they fled. They had no time to gather anything during the Nakba. There was large-scale looting after the city was evacuated.

As we left this house, we saw the rubble from another one across the street that had been recently demolished. We also saw a pile of rubbish that had been left uncollected for days. There were rats.

'I met an old bearded Arab one day near a house that had been gutted and half demolished,' Sarah said. 'I asked him about his life in Jaffa and he offered me his understanding of existence. He saw himself as a single speck in a long historical process that proceeded like a huge wheel that was always moving but so infinitesimally slowly that it looked to each generation as if it were stationery. Only through the perspective of many years can its movement be discerned. My life, he told me, does not matter unless I see it from this broader perspective, in relation to what came before and what will come after. Jaffa, the coast, Acre, Palestine, Syria. One conqueror came, stayed and then was forced to move on. The next conqueror was followed by another, and so on. None have managed to stay for ever. The wheel is constantly moving, but slowly. It never stops turning. I envied the vision of that old man.'

Before I left for Ramallah, Sarah told me of a strange dream she had had, perhaps brought about by my visit:

At first there was a buzzing sound, probably an actual fly in my room. I tried to block it out, but there was another sound, a sort of continuous murmur, low and breathy, the sound of women close by. I strained my ears to listen. I was naked when I left the bed. I walked out on to the porch. There was a group of Palestinian women having their afternoon tea, but they weren't like the Arabs I usually see. They were dressed like they were in the 1930s. They were seated on white wicker chairs around a table covered by a multicoloured embroidered cloth. On it lay neatly cut sandwiches, ginger biscuits, an apple pie and a chocolate cake. One woman was pouring tea out of a shining silver teapot into daintily designed cups. But as the tea struck it, each cup cracked and the pieces shattered over the woman's lap. The others did not seem to notice. They continued with their quiet conversation. One of them had a satin collar. There was a cold breeze that caused the delicate fabric to ruffle and cover the woman's left cheek. She seemed to notice me. She smiled in my direction and I was suddenly aware of my nakedness. I felt cold and exposed and I folded my arms over my breasts. Then I woke up.

It was already afternoon when I left Jaffa. The sun was still strong and the humidity high, though not as high as at night. I had not slept well because of the heat and I could not wait to get back to Ramallah with its cool, dry weather.

I drove slowly along an old British Mandate-period road, narrow and meandering and lined on both sides with eucalyptus trees brought to Palestine from Australia by the British. There were few cars and I enjoyed the scenery, the wide-open spaces so unlike the hilly terrain around Ramallah. Some fourteen kilometres south of Ramle, I saw a nursery and stopped to buy some seedlings to take back with me. I was looking at the wide variety of plants when the proprietor came over and we began talking. We both loved plants and bonded over this. I learned that she was from Canada, had a weak heart and had recently had a pacemaker installed. She had left Canada because she wanted a different sort of life, one where she could stop working so hard and take the time to enjoy things. She had found it here.

'I never continue working while the sun is setting,' she said. 'I leave whatever I'm doing, rush out and just stand there enjoying the scenery. On the plain, we get an unobstructed view of the horizon and an amazing array of colours. Every day it's different.'

As I continued my rounds of the nursery, I saw ruins on the opposite side of the road, evidence of a Palestinian village that had been destroyed. I hadn't noticed them before. A young Palestinian man was working among the plants with a spade and I asked him in Arabic, 'Which village was that?'

He looked up, hesitated, then answered, 'Khirbat Beit Far.'

'Did the inhabitants leave in 1948 or were they evicted afterwards?' I asked. 'And where are they now?'

'Where are they now?' he repeated. 'Scattered all over the globe.' He scrutinised my face, trying to understand where I came from and why I was interrogating him.

'Are you from here?' I asked.

He was from Ramallah but slept at the nursery during the week and returned home at the weekend. He had been working with this woman for five years now. He spoke fluent Hebrew with her and they seemed very friendly and comfortable with each other.

I felt a burst of anger, as though what I had suppressed during my visit to Jaffa was coming to the surface. I felt like asking this middle-aged woman how she could establish her nursery on land expropriated from villagers who were now forced to live in crowded refugee camps with no land to cultivate for themselves. I wanted to shake her out of her equanimity. How could she watch the sunset with an easy conscience when such a tragedy had taken place on the land she now exploits?

I went to find her, but I had a change of heart. Was it the plants that had a calming influence on me? Whatever it was I could not tell her what I had been determined to say. Instead I bought some plants. She smiled at me and gave me a seedling for free.

When I reached the Latrun Monastery, I saw some Palestinian labourers waving at me. They wanted a lift, so I stopped and took in two. On the way they told me that they worked at a nearby factory, starting at six in the morning and finishing at three in the afternoon. 'We wake up at four and leave home at quarter to five,' one of them said, 'with the chicken.' They got this work through the labour exchange office. I asked whether they had the same rights as Israeli workers. They said they thought so but were not sure. They did not know the details and never saw the contract. They knew that deductions were made from their salary but were not sure why. Their employer shouted at them and humiliated them whenever they tried to speak to him.

When we got to the turn-off that went to Khirbatha, they asked me to stop. 'This is our village,' they said.

I would have driven them to their doors but I had no time. I would have liked to see their reception when they arrived home and what they did in the evening. They were probably no more than seventeen but they looked older, worn out. It must be a hard existence.

After I dropped them off, I drove on through the hills back to Ramallah. I was looking with new eyes and noticed, perhaps for the first time, how attractive the landscape was. The lure of far-off Jaffa had blinded me from seeing the beauty of those central hills around Ramallah and beyond in the West Bank, where my father had proposed establishing a Palestinian state.

A whole new world was opening up to me, one that I had remained prejudiced against for so long. My gaze had always been fixed on the horizon, on Jaffa and the coast, and I had failed to see and appreciate what lay closer to home.

4

Naomi

Jerusalem, 1981

In 1981 I was preparing to publish a number of essays that I had written for a London-based magazine, *The Middle East*, under the pseudonym 'Samed'. My Israeli publisher told me he knew a skilled editor and asked whether I would mind working with an Israeli. That was how I met Naomi.

We arranged to meet in East Jerusalem, in the courtyard of the American Colony Hotel, with its small fountain, goldfish pond and palm tree, the fronds forming a canopy over the open space. At that time the hotel was a meeting place for Palestinians and Israelis, and we continued to go there often over the years. The staff were mainly Arabs from Jerusalem and the West Bank. At night a small Israeli jazz band played in the cavernous bar in the basement. The atmosphere was romantic and dreamy.

Naomi was slim, intense and highly intelligent, with beautiful, frank eyes. She had short hair which she continuously swept off her face. Like most other

Israelis, she smoked a lot and played with her cigarette between her fingers.

Her glittering eyes looked at me with affection and bemusement. She was quick to laugh and generous with her laughter. She emphasised her words, choosing them carefully, and had a way of using her hands to make a point – not unlike Arabs, although the gestures were different, especially the way she often used her little finger, which she held apart from her other fingers as if favouring it to make a finer distinction. Different fingers were used to emphasise different points, as if playing the piano in the air. Then she would audibly draw breath, screw up her eyes and gaze into the distance. I liked her.

The daughter of an Israeli diplomat, Naomi had grown up in a number of different countries. When she was drafted into the army she was initially enthusiastic but soon lost interest. She was highly moral. She was concerned about what was taking place around her and willing to speak out. In so many ways she was the opposite of Henry, who remained diffident and reluctant to commit himself, especially when it came to politics.

At the time we met, Naomi was working for the *Jerusalem Post*, where her brother was a night editor. We got along well. At that first meeting Naomi asked me what my book was about and I told her that it was about perseverance (*sumoud*) and explained what this meant, how it was a strategy of civil resistance. We Palestinians decided to stay put despite all the efforts of the occupiers to make life difficult for us in order to encourage us to leave. I made sure to emphasise that it was not about politics. She looked sceptical. When I explained that I had a hatred of politics, she laughed. I went on to say that I was writing about daily life and how to survive – how to develop a Palestinian community even under occupation.

'And this is not politics?' she gently enquired.

I insisted that it wasn't. I gave her the manuscript and we parted, but not before planning to meet again at her home in the German Colony in West Jerusalem.

Next day I went to her house. It had an attractive front porch and was surrounded on all sides by a garden. The front garden had a few shrubs but was not cultivated. It was at the back of the house that Naomi's mother applied her energy. Different annuals were planted there, each season producing a sea of joyful colour. Her mother, who took the Hebrew name Rosheen when she married Naomi's father, was English and a superb gardener. They had a dog which they had found sick and lame in the gutter. They spoke to him in Hebrew.

I soon discovered that Naomi and I agreed about the danger of building settlements and the desperate need to speak out before it was too late. We were kindred spirits. At the time I was investigating the illegal ways in which the settlers had registered a local company to circumvent prevailing Jordanian law prohibiting the sale of land to foreigners without permission from a local authority. Meanwhile, messianic rabbis, such as Zvi Yehuda Kook, were claiming that the settlement of the land was by divine command. I

remember wondering what could be so divine about
a process that was proceeded by stealth and illegality.
But I still had faith that secular law would eventually
be enforced. Al-Haq's publications documented what
was taking place and its effect on Palestinian farmers.
One of the publications was a collection of statements
under oath from those whose human rights had been
violated which we called *In Their Own Words*. Naomi's
mother, Rosheen, helped to edit it. It included testi-
monies from farmers whose land had been confiscated
for the building of settlements or whose houses had
been pulled down or sealed by the military, people who
had been placed under town arrest and academics who
had suffered censorship, harassment and the closure of
their universities.

I was anxious. I could see disaster looming in the
not too distant future if nothing was done immediately to stop the violations, especially those against
the new generation of Palestinians. Evidently, while
encouraging these settlements to prosper, the Israeli
military authorities pursued a policy of stifling Palestinian development by refusing to grant permits vital
for building the necessary infrastructure for invest-
ment and economic progress. I wasted no opportunity
to speak out or write about these disastrous policies,
which I believed would only hamper and complicate the
resolution of the conflict. I was confident that Al-Haq's
work and the book I was working on would awaken
others in Israel and abroad to what was happening.

As the deadline for the manuscript approached, I
spent a lot of time with Naomi discussing the order of

the pieces and making extensive changes. I completely trusted her opinion, had faith in her skills as an editor and thoroughly enjoyed working with her. A strong personal friendship grew between us that has never since been broken.

That year, 1981, was a time of change and not for the better. Israel reneged on the promise it had made to US president Jimmy Carter not to build more Jewish settlements in the West Bank. Prime Minister Menachem Begin, who was religious, must have reasoned that it was more important to follow the will of God than a promise to a secular president – not to mention that it was politically more expedient for his party, Likud, to pursue the colonisation of Palestinian territory and make available free land for his electorate. As the Camp David negotiations proceeded over the fate of the West Bank and the Gaza Strip, it was becoming clear that in return for Sinai and the neutralisation of Egypt, Israel was giving itself the West Bank. Anwar Sadat, whose words had given me hope, did not follow through on what he had promised.

On 2 June a year earlier, the Jewish Underground, a terrorist group formed by militants in the settler movement, tried to assassinate the mayors of Bireh, Nablus and Ramallah in the West Bank by planting bombs in their cars. Bassam Shakaa, the mayor of Nablus, lost his legs, and it was reported that on hearing the news Rabbi Haim Drukman, co-founder of the extremist settler movement Gush Emunim (Bloc of the Faithful) and later a member of the Knesset and Deputy Minister of Religious Affairs, sang a line from the Song of Deborah: 'Thus may all Israel's enemies perish.'

I remember the first time I read about Gush Emunim. It was 1978, one year after Begin was elected prime minister of Israel. The victory of the hawkish, right-wing Likud party after thirty years in opposition was considered an upheaval in the political life of the state. It ended the hegemony of the Labour party, which was mainly led by Ashkenazi Jews. Likud was openly committed to establishing more settlements in the West Bank and holding on to Jerusalem, including the Arab eastern side of the city, as the 'eternal capital' of Israel. My first thought was that the Gush Emunim was a delusional fringe group. I was not alone. In 1976 Prime Minister Yitzhak Rabin gave an interview in which he compared the settlements to 'a cancer in the social and democratic tissue of the State of Israel'. He criticised Gush Emunim as 'a group that takes the law into its own hands'.

At that time I didn't think the organisation posed a real threat. How could they force us out? Are we not persevering (*samdeen*)? Unlike in 1948, we didn't leave our homes when the war erupted in 1967. '*Sumoud*,' I wrote, 'is our collective way of challenging the occupation. Whatever the Israeli military does to make us leave, we will not go.' I was encouraged by Rabin, who said in that same interview that 'because of the [Arab] population I don't think it will be possible to [settle] over time unless we want to get to apartheid, with a million and a half Arabs inside the State of Israel'. But as the number of settlements grew, I realised that while they might be deranged they were serious and they had the support of the Likud government under Begin, which took over in 1977. Begin was no champion of peace or of reconciliation with the Palestinian people. He refused to recognise that the Palestinians were a people. In an article published in 1970 in the Israeli daily *Maariv*, Begin had made his position known:

> If a Jew, or a Zionist, a minister or spokesman, acknowledges the Palestinisation of the Jewish–Arab conflict, he still has no authority to determine that Israel ends here and Palestine begins there, or vice versa. He has accepted our enemies' main argument. He has betrayed that of his own people. If this be the Land of Israel, we have returned to it. If it is Palestine, we have invaded it. If Eretz Israel it be, we have established legitimate rule throughout it; if it be Palestine, our rule is not legitimate in any area of it.

Month by month, the nightmare grew as more and more Jewish settlements were established. My father was right when he said that time was of the essence. If we waited too long the establishment of a Palestinian state would no longer be viable. As the settlements advanced and more land was taken using means that we were helpless to stop through legal action, I became more certain that the policy of the Israeli government was to throw us out altogether. All this was to make room for Jews from the West, like Henry.

The spring after Naomi and I finished editing the manuscript, there was turmoil in the occupied West Bank, mainly involving settler violence. But she and I continued to meet. That summer she was due to travel to England to continue her studies in philosophy, so we decided to go to my family's house in Jericho to celebrate the book's completion. There in that oasis we could escape, however briefly, from everything.

Time seemed to stop there. It was March and the citrus orchards were in blossom. As we entered Jericho we were embraced by their fragrance. In the garden of my family's house we built a small fire and set up a table that we covered with a checked tablecloth. We drank champagne and ate grilled white goat's cheese, roasted almonds and pistachios. We were alone – alone without any soldiers nearby – under a sky studded with stars.

Afterwards we strolled in the garden to the pomelo tree, stooping down to smell its blossoms, which looked like white nipples in the still darkness. We stretched out on the grass under the tree, staring up at the stars between the branches. I closed my eyes and when I opened them again I wondered for a moment where I was. I felt so utterly at one with everything around me, out of space and time, absorbed by my senses. We had left behind all our troubles and entered paradise. We remained there on the grass for what felt like an eternity, then returned to the house. The next day was the same – undisturbed by the world outside.

Before leaving Jericho, I bought Naomi and her mother flowerpots and seedlings for the garden. I remember Naomi holding them in both hands as I drove to her mother's place. But the first thing her mother asked was, 'Why didn't you tell me you were going for twenty-four hours?' I had felt her anger, her reproach, and did not stay.

On the outskirts of Ramallah, there was a prominent stop sign. As I approached, an Israeli soldier motioned with his torchlight for me to stop. It was like entering a large prison camp. The soldier asked for my identity card and I gave it to him. I thought of asking him for the latest news but stopped myself. It felt strange asking an Israeli soldier to tell me what had happened in my hometown. The soldier with the yarmulke ordered me to wait on the side of the road. Time passed slowly. After obediently waiting for an hour, I called the soldier and asked him why I could not go home. He took out a piece of paper, which he read to me. It said that a curfew had been imposed on Ramallah by order of the military commander of the West Bank.

I felt a twinge in my stomach. 'I want to go home,' I said. But the soldier, this foreigner, was not moved. 'Go back to where you came from,' he ordered. I could not return.

I did not know then that worse was yet to happen, for on 6 June 1982 Israel declared war on the PLO in Lebanon. This was to be the first of many invasions. These events seemed to mock everything I had written. The degree of violence and of evil was far worse than anything I had been trying to discuss in my 'Samed' pieces.

Ever an incorrigible optimist, I underestimated the level of Israel's brutality against the Palestinians in Lebanon. Naomi knew better. She had no illusions about her own people and had not been as sure as I was that all would turn out well. She expressed surprise at my inability to see the dark side of Israel's policy, which to her was self-evident.

Soon after the invasion of Lebanon, I visited Naomi at her home. It was a glorious, sunny day and her mother was hard at work in the garden. 'My mother has decided to go all out this year. She's planting sixty-five petunia seedlings. In a month the place will be awash with colour.' Then she told me how the front garden used to be full of cyclamen at this time of year but they had all gone because some rodent had eaten the bulbs.

I observed how carefully Rosheen, with her high cheekbones and beautiful, intelligent blue eyes, carried out her task, kneeling on the bare earth, digging a hole, pouring in a little compost and placing the seedling in the hole. She was a committed gardener and seemed to be thoroughly enjoying her work. Watching her, I almost forgot the pain I felt about the war raging in Lebanon. I began to feel guilty about losing myself in the beauty of a garden in West Jerusalem when my own people were suffering in the refugee camps in Lebanon.

Three weeks after the war had started I took Naomi for a walk in the Ramallah hills. As the sun was setting, we sat on the rocks in the wadi, an enchanting view of the hills in front of us. In the distance we could hear a loudspeaker on an Israeli jeep playing Lebanese folk-songs sung by Druze soldiers and *mawals* in Arabic. As we walked back, the sky above us was crimson and pink – it is the sun that gives colour and beauty to all things. On the way down, clusters of spindly brooms with their yellow flowers glittered and shone in the dimming light like lanterns. On the top of one of the hills, the silhouettes of olive trees assumed the shapes of animals and people. While we walked, Naomi told me what she had seen on the Israeli news about the things that were happening in Lebanon. As I listened, I became aware that I had avoided confronting the full horror that was unfolding there just as I had avoided confronting my misgivings about my friend Henry.

In the spring of that year, I went hiking in Wadi Qelt, near Jericho, for the first time. The land was blooming and after the heavy rains the waterfalls were strong and the water in the wadi ran like a river. When I reached the Monastery of St George of Koziba, in the narrowest part of the gorge, I passed an Israeli soldier and thought of a note I had received from Henry. He had been travelling abroad and had written to say we should get together on his return home. Israel as home. It gave me pause. Henry was not born in Israel. He had come of his own free will. Didn't he need to make known his objection to what his adopted country was doing to the Palestinians? He insisted he would never join the army, but was this enough? Wasn't he confirming by the mere act of moving here that Zionism was working and that the settlements were justified?

On another occasion, I was driving to Jerusalem, admiring the hills, their slopes cultivated with olive trees, the morning sun giving the leaves a grey-green hue. It also made me think of Henry. How could the settlers see this and think it was uninhabited? Such is the blinding power of religion. Did Henry, a constant reader of the Bible, have similarly distorted vision?

I imagined confronting Henry with this.

He would say, 'This is an abuse of religion. It is not at all how I see Judaism. I'm against Jewish settlements in the Occupied Territories and support the call for a Palestinian state. It is true that I am here as a Jew, but not as a colonialist, and I will never tolerate the wrong done to Palestinians. I am your friend and want us to live together as brothers. Don't you see the difference? The existence of a Jewish home is important to me, but I don't want it to oppress Palestinians and deny them their human rights. I want us to live together.'

And I would reply, 'But your very presence here is because you're a Jew. This fact alone gives you more rights to this country than I have. The Jewish presence in this land has turned out to be not just cultural, as you had hoped. It is a colonising presence. Can you not see this?'

It is what one brings to a place that determines one's experience of it, not just what is there. Henry brought with him his mother's yearning to settle in Israel. She was a Zionist, but she did have serious misgivings about Israel and, unlike her sister, she had delayed bringing her family over. Henry's mother had expressed her objections to him about how the Israeli government was behaving, but he wanted to make it a better place to live – not through political action but through human interaction. Henry had thought he would be involved in politics, but he realised that it would get him into trouble so he stayed away.

When Henry read the manuscript of my book of essays, he liked it. He shared my belief in *sumoud*. He told me that in the Treblinka concentration camp the inmates would say, 'Faced with two alternatives, always choose the third.' I appreciated the aphorism, expanded it and used it for the back cover of the book, adding, 'Between mute submission and blind hate, I choose the third way. I am Samed.' This was how the book found its title, *The Third Way*. I was gaining more clarity about my attitude to what was taking place around me and how to represent it, but I was failing to find a way to express these apprehensions that I felt about Henry.

Every day, I received reports of the terrible things being done to the Palestinians by Begin's government, but Henry reassured me that Begin was not representative of all Israelis. Jews have a morality that will ultimately deter them, he assured me. I thought about this as I once again stood in an office, delayed, humiliated, asking the military for some permit or other. What use was this morality when its existence meant my daily suffering? Had Henry spoken out against any of this?

Henry gave me many things I was looking for

in a friendship. We spoke of books. We talked about ourselves. We enjoyed walking. I liked his sense of humour. I told myself that there was no reason why he should be an activist. Did everyone here have to be an activist? So many self-proclaimed activists did not interest me. I liked Henry for who he was and this was enough. It was wrong to expect Henry to be political when it wasn't in his nature to be so.

I was returning from a visit to my sisters in Amman when I met Henry's friend Eldad at the Allenby Bridge. With his frog-like eyes and drooping face, he was easy to recognise. When we'd first met – at dinner at the house of Henry's girlfriend, Iva – he had seemed perfectly agreeable and pleasant, but this time he was wearing an army uniform. His reserve duty consisted of searching Palestinian passengers crossing the bridge between Jordan and Israel. We were no longer fellow guests at a dinner party; we were now a civilian from an occupied population and a soldier in the occupying army.

Eldad proceeded to exercise the full authority afforded by his status and his uniform. The search was humiliating and, throughout it all, he didn't even pretend not to know me. He talked about the dinner party, how he had enjoyed meeting me there and then ordered me to take off my belt and shoes, lower my trousers, spread my legs and turn around. He ordered me to empty my bag. Any questionable items he threw in a basket to be confiscated, including the presents I had brought back for my mother, a tin of Tiger Balm and several cakes of perfumed soap. He made no apologies. I remained silent. He could tell I was angry.

'I have to follow the rules,' he said.

When I told Henry of this encounter he did not seem unduly perturbed. It made me wonder whether, when the time came, he also would be willing to follow orders.

While the war continued in Lebanon, I travelled to London and Oxford on Al-Haq business to meet Amnesty International and Oxfam. Afterwards I took time off to walk in the Lake District. From there I wrote Henry a letter:

Dear Henry,

Harsh words, but I feel I must say them. I strongly believe anyone, whether a citizen or living here as you do and participating in the life of the state and its 'development', is a victim of the evil just as I am. However, inasmuch as you have made your choice to come to Israel and settle, by your silence you are acquiescing and participating in its evil. I can never respect you for that, nor forgive you. The absence of your voice against what is taking place in Lebanon with the Israeli army has cut me deeply. I mistrusted my attitude and thought that travelling abroad would make me change it. But being away only confirmed my stance.

All this has made me realise how totally devastating it is for a friendship when one loses one's respect for his friend, as I have. It did not have to be so. Ours was a strong tie, with strong beliefs and expectations. The disappointment is equally strong.

I thought of you every time I stopped – especially when sitting on the hill by Lake Windermere in England – but my feelings persisted and persist now. I find it difficult to change my expectations, to redefine my relationship and understanding of you.

I am as sorry for you as I am for myself. Our only common denominator is that we are both victims of evil. The sooner you admit this the healthier it would be for you. I sincerely wish it for both our sakes.

Several nights ago, I dreamed that you came over. You had shaved your beard. It was difficult to recognise you. You had to introduce yourself to me. Yours was a boyish face but a tired, less handsome one than your own, also thinner.

I found myself having to make your acquaintance anew. Around your neck you wore a medallion of a royal-blue colour. That was your only distinction. I remember thinking you wore it to replace the gap left by the shaved beard. Then you walked away. I called you, but you were running away with a smile on your face.

I only thought I owe it to you, to our friendship, to let you know how deeply disappointed I feel. At the end of the day I did not know now whether to be happy, relieved or regretful at the loss of your beard.

Henry's response saddened me. He tried to reaffirm our friendship outside politics and refused to respond to my challenge on 'such a political level'. Instead he tried to explain how important it was for him to come to Israel, the place where his late mother had dreamed of coming. He was living her dream and in this way keeping her alive. He wanted this to be an individual act without any political significance.

On 7 July 1982 he again wrote to me:

Raja,

Today one of my patients, a woman I have been seeing for a year, told me that if things don't change in the next six months or so she will commit suicide. What do you say to a person in despair – that nevertheless there is meaning?

But as Henry, as Enoch the Jew, I do feel that I am murdering your people here daily with frightening efficiency, and will I, can I, live up to those expectations of which you write so beautifully? For I think you are right. I have failed you – my demonstrations, proclamations, against the occupation don't help you or your people a damn.

Still, Raja my friend, my Palestinian, I do love you and cherish this thing which has grown between us. I feel I should respond to you and your tale. But I am unable now to do it on such a political level. I will send you a fantasy which started from a dream so that even at some level we can remain in dialogue. Or perhaps, as your dream suggests, shave my beard …

And finally, although you will get a formal invitation, I do want to add that Iva and I will be married on 12 August at 5 p.m. at Rehov Hakevet 53 (along railway tracks) and I hope you will come. *Fiddler on the Roof*,

which I recall you like, has a line: Life has so much
suffering, a wedding gives us an excuse if only for a little
while to rejoice.

Yours,
Enoch

What worried me was his designation in a letter,
signed using his biblical name, of me as 'my Palestinian'. Could I be, as I had sometimes suspected, a token
Palestinian friend? The mere suspicion that this might
be the case troubled me. Our friendship was more profound and closer than that. And yet this reference led
me to worry and suspect. I would never have called
him 'my Jew' or 'my Israeli'. To me Henry was too
much of an individual for that.

A few days later Henry visited me. He brought
with him the formal invitation to his wedding to Iva.
It was the first meeting between us in many months.
He told me he was trying to make his wedding a happy
event where all would feel welcome, communal and
close. Call it childish, call it selfish, call it indulgence,
he said, but life must go on. 'We must find time to
marry, time to be merry, even during periods of great
disaster and horror. As is the case now,' he told me.

After he left I realised that this was Henry the
dreamer, the anthropologist, the carefree man, the
modern Jew. He was no moralist, not someone who
claimed the moral high ground. Nor was he one who
could assume responsibility or feel responsible for
what was being done in the name of his religion. He

had his own very special conception of what being Jewish was. I could not expect more of him and perhaps it was unfair that I did.

I attended Henry and Iva's wedding despite the war in the north and its venue in an old Palestinian home. It turned out to be a joyful event, everything that Henry had hoped it would be, and it brought together a diverse community of friends.

That summer Naomi went back to Oxford to pursue her studies. On 16 September her worst fears about Sharon materialised in the form of massacres at two Palestinian refugee camps, Sabra and Shatila, in Beirut. Over the course of two days thousands of mostly Palestinians and Shiite Lebanese were killed when Israeli troops under Sharon's leadership allowed their Phalangist allies to enter the camps under the light of Israeli flares.

A week later I received a postcard from Henry:

Only now hearing about the Lebanese massacres. There is nothing to say. I bow my head in shame and pray for the consolation of prayer.

Your friend,
Henry

5

The Sea

Akka, 1971

When the occupation began in 1967 the whole of what had been Mandatory Palestine was opened to us for the first time since the establishment of Israel nineteen years earlier. The Israeli military government declared the West Bank a closed military zone and issued a general permit that allowed the Palestinians to cross into Israel. Prior to this we in the West Bank had had no access to the sea, but now the Mediterranean became a mere hour's drive away from Ramallah. It was so close we couldn't get enough of it. We began driving there every week in summer. Akka (Acre), Jaffa, Haifa – I liked to repeat the names of the coastal cities, and I could hardly believe they were now within easy reach. The sea was ours again and the land acquired a new integrity, a completeness that I had not felt previously.

It isn't that we didn't go to the sea before that. We used to make the arduous journey every summer to the Mediterranean but further north, on the shores of

Lebanon. It would take more than eight hours by car – from Jordan through Syria and then to Lebanon – to reach our destination. At each border, we never knew whether we would be allowed to cross.

Every Sunday during the summer in the first few years of occupation we would leave Ramallah early in the morning. We drove through Betunia, took the Latrun road and crossed the central hills to the coastal plain. My father's driving often made us queasy. He would take corners fast and brake all too suddenly. We could hardly wait to get to the straight roads on the plain. Once there, we enjoyed being close to the sea, feeling the sea air blowing through the open windows of the white Mercedes in which all six of us were crammed.

At first we used to go to the beaches closer to Ramallah, such as Bat Yam, south of Jaffa, which could be reached in around forty-five minutes. At Bat Yam there was usually a group of older retired men, Arabs and Jews, veterans of the sea. The Arabs who remained in Palestine after 1948 had thick, tanned salamander skin. Wearing only black trunks and unselfconscious about their nakedness, they sat on low stools playing backgammon, or *shish besh*, thumping the pieces down on the board. I wanted to be like them and wondered whether I would have been if my father had stayed in Jaffa and we'd lived close to the sea. How much time would I have needed to spend at the beach to get that kind of skin?

We discovered that the ancient port city of Akka had a superb area for swimming. The city is surrounded by a formidable wall that was first constructed in the ninth century by Ahmad Ibn Tulun, who ordered that it be made as impregnable as Tyre. This did not prevent its conquest by the Crusaders in 1104, who left an impressive underground city with seven large halls and a tunnel that now leads to a Turkish hammam. The city had beautiful churches, mosques and khans, but we did not go there to visit the ruins or the places of worship. Our main interest was swimming. Most weekends in the summer we would drive some four hours to dip in the placid waters of Akka's natural bay. We would take an elaborate picnic basket of delicious snacks, pastries of all sorts, nuts, fried courgettes and aubergines, salty white goat's cheese, tomatoes, cucumbers and sliced watermelon, and have fried fish for lunch. We felt safe there.

In the cold winter months we packed our overnight bags and went to stay in Tiberias on the Sea of Galilee at the old Scots Hotel, which had served as a hospital under the British Mandate. My mother's uncle had worked there as a pharmacist and my grandmother Julia had been born there. It still had the gong they used to strike to announce that breakfast was being served. At the time we used to visit, my eldest sister, Siham, was studying at Beirut College for Women. We were warned not to write to her about our trips to Tiberias in case the letter fell into the hands of the Lebanese authorities. Lebanon was still at war with Israel and they would have seen our visits as suspicious. Instead we would write that we had spent the night at our grandmother's birthplace.

Both Jaffa, my father's city, and Akka, where his sister, Mary, lived with her family, were to be part of the Arab state under the 1947 United Nations Partition Plan for Palestine, which divided Palestine into an Arab and a Jewish state. This was why, in the spring of 1948, my father was not against spending the beginning of the family's usual summer holiday in Ramallah, away from humid Jaffa. By April it had become too dangerous to stay in Jaffa and the British police, who were still in control, would not protect the local Arab population. My father also believed that he would be able to return once the partition scheme had been implemented.

On 18 May 1948 Akka fell to Israeli forces, a few days after they had taken Jaffa. By then only 3,000 out of the 13,560 Palestinian inhabitants of the city remained. The others had been forced to flee, some on foot to the eastern hills, some by boat to Tyre and Beirut. But Mary could not leave. Her youngest daughter, Amal, was only a few years old and she had typhoid. They feared for her life if they left.

Mary and her family were forced out of their home and, along with the remaining Palestinians, were confined in a small section of the Old City that they could leave only with the permission of the occupying Israeli forces. There they heard about a massacre of some seventy Palestinians. Many now regretted their decision to stay, but there was a strong sense of solidarity and cooperation among them. Mary's daughter survived.

There was little opportunity for communication at

first between my father and his sister but eventually they were able to exchange letters through the Red Cross. Often my father's letters included the words *ana jai*, I'm coming, as he held on to his belief that he would somehow return home. He had tried. He knew the road to Jaffa from Ramallah was open and he tried to organise for the refugees to return to their city, but the Jordanian soldiers came for him and he was taken to prison, where he spent a few nights.

After his release, he travelled independently of the Jordanian authorities to Lausanne with a small delegation representing the refugees to negotiate with the newly established Israeli government. His goal was for the return of the refugees to Palestine and compensation for those who did not. But Israel refused to have anything to do with them. We are now a state, they declared, and will negotiate only with other states.

My father returned disappointed. He tried to go back to Jaffa with his family and a few friends. But these efforts came to nothing and he remained in that small house in Ramallah, where he and his growing family shared a few rooms with his difficult mother-in-law. On clear evenings he could see the city on the horizon.

Still he continued to write to his sister. Still with the hopeful words *ana jai*.

Did these letters comfort Mary? She had always looked to her older brother for support and the two of them had endured a great deal together. Their mother died when they were still only a few years old in the typhus epidemic during the First World War. Their devastated father took care of them on his own until he married a young woman also called Mary. My aunt Mary was sent to a boarding school in Bethlehem, but my father lived at home.

Perhaps my father's letters gave my aunt some hope that her beloved brother would return and that she would not remain cut off from him, on her own, in the newly created State of Israel. But the promise of *ana jai* never came to anything and the two were unable to meet for many years, until in 1956 Israel agreed to allow some of the Christian Arabs to visit their holy places and their relatives for forty-eight hours on Christmas in what became the West Bank.

Then one day in 1961 word came to my father that his sister had died of complications due to diabetes, from which my father also suffered. He had been unable to say farewell; he was not even able to attend her funeral.

By the time it was possible to visit Akka again, after 1967, all my cousins except the youngest, Nuha, had found a future for themselves away from Israel, where opportunities for them were so restricted. Mary's widower, Abu Naseef, lived with his youngest daughter, who was still in school. I grew up without knowing, without even meeting, any of my male cousins in Akka. When, several years later, we met in the United States, they were strangers to me.

One of my earliest memories of Akka is a trip we took with a radiologist friend of my father, Khalil Jubran, a bon vivant with a dimpled chin and sparkling eyes, and his lively wife, Sumaya. The water was calm and we all floated on our backs under the strong August sun. I remember hearing Khalil mutter to himself, 'Could there be a better place than this? This is heaven.'

In a few years Khalil had left the area. He had asked my father how he would find husbands for his five daughters there. He emigrated to Jacksonville, Florida, joining scores of other middle-class Palestinian families from Ramallah. There he qualified as an anaesthetist, practising for a number of years before he died of a heart attack. I remember thinking that if this brain drain continued there would be no one left.

The spirit of *sumoud* had not yet taken root. A number of families from Ramallah had left during the 1967 war, fearing that their young daughters would be raped. Now more were leaving in the hope that their daughters would have better marriage prospects. As for sons, fathers feared that they might join the Palestinian resistance and end up either killed or imprisoned by the Israeli authorities.

Once they had left Ramallah, the Jubrans never returned, not even for a visit. To save their beautiful home, with its arched balcony in front and its glorious garden, my father had a relative of ours and his family live there so that the occupying army would not take it over as abandoned property. After Khalil's death, his daughters sold the house in Ramallah through power of attorney. They never set foot in their country again and the house was subsequently demolished to make way for an ugly shopping mall.

Under the Israeli occupation, more and more of Ramallah's original inhabitants emigrated. The vast majority of them sold their homes and their land, severing all ties with their city. Most didn't bother to teach their children Arabic. One after another, the old attractive houses were destroyed by their new owners, who had no feeling for the city. Consequently, little remains of the old Ramallah and the new city feels characterless. The inevitable development took place without any attempt at preserving Ramallah's original charm. Instead, it was destroyed for ever.

Today when I think of Khalil Jubran I remember him in the garden of the Grand Hotel in Ramallah, where he used to get together with my father and spend long afternoons relaxing, joking and telling stories. One of these stories was about how he once stopped his car – he was a notoriously slow driver – on the way to Jerusalem, where he worked at the Augusta Victoria Hospital, for a woman who needed a lift. She refused his offer, saying (and here he would smile his impish smile), 'Thank you, doctor, but I'm in a hurry.'

Those sorts of leisurely, genial gatherings are now rare. After five decades of occupation and the destruction of old Ramallah, most faces are sombre and burdened. Perhaps this is not unique to Palestine, but unlike places such as Italy and Greece ours is a bitter maturity. Instead of gaiety there is empty laughter masquerading as the real thing.

For the first two decades under the occupation, the borders between Israel and the West Bank remained porous, but with the start of the first intifada in 1987 more blockades and checkpoints appeared on the roads. New roads were constructed to ensure speedy passage between the Jewish settlements in the West Bank and Israel. It was not until the signing of the Oslo Accord in 1993 that Israel began drawing a new border between Israel and the West Bank that prevented access from Palestinian cities and villages while allowing the unobstructed flow of traffic between the West Bank Jewish settlements and Israel. The general permit issued in 1967 for Palestinians to move to and from Israel was replaced by individual permits, allowing access only to those Palestinians whom Israel deemed favourable. Once again we were prevented from visiting the sea.

6

The Bougainvillea

Ramallah, 1988

About two months after the beginning of the first intifada, we were sitting together, the staff of Al-Haq and I, in a small meeting room, talking about the shootings, the beatings, the arrests, the curfews, the demolition of houses and the economic sanctions taking place in the West Bank. Since the minister of defence, Yitzhak Rabin, like a stern father reprimanding his unruly children, had announced his policy of 'force, might and beatings', our usual method of operation had been rendered obsolete.

For many years, we had taken the Israeli government at its word – that it did not deliberately violate human rights as a policy, that abuses were an exception. Conscious of the international public's scepticism of what a Palestinian organisation might say about Israel, we presented the violations to the Israeli authorities and they would respond by challenging our findings or by justifying their actions, claiming that they were consistent with the law. Often they said these actions were necessary for security. So how could we now approach a government that had declared in the clearest possible manner that its agents would use force, whose soldiers had fired in the first two weeks of the intifada some 1.2 million bullets – about 100,000 a day – that had killed several dozen Palestinians and injured many more?

How could we have imagined that a time would come when thousands of soldiers would pass through towns, villages and refugee camps in the West Bank and the Gaza Strip, breaking all accepted human rights norms, stopping passers-by and humiliating them, beating them or detaining them, shooting at unarmed demonstrators and imposing long-term curfews on entire communities under the orders of their highest-ranking officers? What was the point of producing another report when this was well-known throughout the world? What was the role of a human rights organisation at a time like this?

As the discussions continued without conclusion, we heard a loud cry from the street. We dropped everything and rushed to the balcony.

Two soldiers stood opposite our building.

'What happened?' called Jonathan Kuttab, the co-director of Al-Haq, in Hebrew.

The soldiers did not answer but gestured to three other soldiers who were standing right under our balcony. The five moved on. Then we saw a young man emerge from the door of our building carrying his shopping in a plastic bag. His face was bleeding.

Riziq, one of our researchers, rushed down the

three flights of stairs to catch up with him. The rest of us followed. On the way down, we saw a small puddle of blood on one of the landings.

The young man had disappeared. Riziq walked into a gym across the street to ask if anyone had seen him. It was a stuffy little room smelling of sweat and filled with young men lifting weights and learning self-defence. They said they hadn't seen him.

It was dark now in the streets. There wasn't a soul outside. Riziq tried other houses and eventually found the young man and brought him and his brother to Al-Haq. Our cameras were ready to document his injuries. While some of us tended to his wounds, the young man cursed vociferously, his brother too, but their anger was directed against us.

'Human rights? If soldiers can beat a man in your own stairwell and you can do nothing about it, why are you here at all?' they said.

We were silent.

The young man explained that he had been returning home with his groceries when he was met by the five soldiers near our door. They must have thought this was an empty building because they shoved him into the doorway, then dropped something on the floor and told him to pick it up. When he bent down, one of the soldiers kicked him in the face. That was when he cried out. They were not finished with him, but when they heard movement upstairs they stopped and let him go.

Now we had the facts – an example of how the Rabin policy was being implemented. Jonathan and I left the others and decided to go after the soldiers. We caught up with them at the Manara roundabout in the centre of town, where they had stopped another young man. They recognised us.

'We saw what you did,' we said.

'What did you see?' asked one of the younger soldiers.

A tall soldier with a drooping moustache intervened at that point, asking, 'Who are you?'

We introduced ourselves.

'What do you want?' he said.

'Your names and the name of your unit.'

He looked at us with the full authority of a soldier who knows he has the law on his side. He waved his baton before our eyes and said, 'If you don't leave immediately, I will arrest you. You are interfering with our work.'

I breathed in, feeling as though I was about to explode.

We then decided to try the police station and so started to drive. We drove down the dark, deserted streets under the orange street lights. This was the town where I had grown up. How had it changed so much? It felt so different now, haunted by criminals with orders to wound and even kill.

We parked the car on a side street and walked to the Israeli police station in the centre of Ramallah. A tall pine tree loomed dark above us. This was the road to my old school. This was the bougainvillea I had walked by every day to and from school. Why did it now seem so menacing?

We saw a soldier standing next to the police station relieving himself, his face, unashamedly, turned towards us. A bus full of soldiers was parked nearby. Alongside it was an army jeep. Altogether there were at least forty soldiers there. Jonathan and I were the only people not in uniform, but the soldiers did not pay us any attention. From the bus came voices. They were chanting, '*Rotseem cola*' ('We want cola'). Soldiers came in and out of the building. We could hear screams from inside. It was like a nightmare.

'Who are you?' an officer asked us.

I wanted to leave this little Israel and go back to my Palestinian town, but I couldn't. I didn't want Jonathan to answer. I was afraid. This was not the time to say we were lawyers, not the time to test the system.

'Let's go,' I said to Jonathan.

Jonathan stayed put. He told the soldier who we were and why we were here: to complain.

Complain – fill out forms, provide a statement, leave our names and credentials, have policemen investigate the scene of the crime. What was the point? Would they even bother to write anything down?

But Jonathan persisted. He repeated to the officer that we had witnessed a criminal offence. We had seen the guilty parties. We had come to report it. We wanted to submit a formal complaint for a police investigation.

Meanwhile the soldiers from the bus continued to chant, 'We want cola, we want cola,' now accompanied by the thumping of their heavy boots on the floor.

'Just do me a favour and leave,' the officer said. 'Leave!' he shouted, pushing us away.

And so we left. We had no alternative.

It was in the same building, the Ramallah police station, that twelve years later two Israeli soldiers would be lynched in the second, more violent intifada. The Israeli army, in retaliation, blew up the Ottoman building with a one-ton bomb dropped from the sky by an Israeli helicopter gunship. The building was reduced to rubble, the bougainvillea destroyed.

For now, though, that visit to the Ramallah police station was followed by days marked out by their intensity, full of strong emotion and determination to do all we could.

I went for lunch at my mother's mainly to keep her company. Nearly four years earlier my father had been returning home from his office when he was murdered in the driveway of their house by a collaborator working for Israel. Much as we tried to get the Israeli authorities to investigate properly and bring the perpetrator to justice, our efforts failed and no one was ever charged with my father's murder. Although the horrific event had taken place four years ago, my mother remained inconsolable. Not only had the Israeli police still not arrested the murderer, but I suspected the government was relieved by the death of a moderate peace-seeker like my father. His death marked for me the end of my expectation of a peaceful settlement.

I had done all I could to pursue the investigation and keep it going. My mother was drowning in her own despair. I worried that if I was not careful she would pull me down with her. After one of our lunches I napped on the sofa in the sunshine on my mother's glass balcony. Every so often my head would jerk from dreams and emotions of fear. I was so angry. I would ruminate over the wider implications of the conflict and my response to it.

Israel was fighting for the retention of this land. We were fighting to end the occupation in accordance with international law, which gave us the right to resist. That was how I saw it. I knew I could potentially be drawn into a bitter fight that would cause further bloodshed and suffering. It would require more endurance than I had been capable of before. I could no longer be just an observer. My anger, my sense of duty and of justice, would not allow it.

And yet I felt that to fight in that way was not my role. I should write. It was good to take part in a common struggle, but I knew I should be careful of how far I allowed myself to get involved. I mistrusted my ability to remain restrained. I could not trust myself to face this cruelty and stay sane. By the end of each day I felt so exhausted. I would go home to my one-room flat and sit in the dark, then take a shower, put on my pyjamas and work on updating my book, *Occupier's Law*, on the legal and human rights implications of the occupation.

The day after the one I'd spent agonising at my mother's, I went to the headquarters of the Israeli Civil Administration for the West Bank at Beit El for two trademark objection cases. Working on intellectual property matters was part of our office's commercial practice. As I approached the building, I thought how strange it must appear to those who do not live here that, even in such troubled times, work continues on such mundane problems as trademark registration. I had always wondered how my father had dealt with rental dispute cases at his office in Jaffa just a few weeks before the Nakba. But life goes on until disaster strikes. Law reports under the British Mandate show that the courts were hearing all kinds of disputes until the very end. How could people be so concerned about their petty squabbles when their lives were going to be turned upside down? But there again how could they have known what was coming?

At the gate a young soldier was listening to jazz. Around him were jazz magazines in English and Hebrew. He had the radio volume turned up high. There was another, older soldier there with a beard. He looked fierce and was pacing around, seemingly bored.

'Close the door,' the young soldier ordered.

I turned to the open door closest to me.

'No, not that one. The one over there.'

'It's not my duty here to close doors,' I said.

'I said, "Close the door."'

I stood my ground.

'You don't want to close the door?'

I shrugged my shoulders. I was calm on the surface but inside I was boiling with rage – rage at being ordered about in any way, at any time, for any reason, by any soldier, young or old, because he was a soldier with a gun and therefore had the authority. Or was it self-loathing for being afraid, weak, easily provoked?

'I'll close the door,' the older soldier said.

The young soldier began looking in his book. He was checking whether I was on a black list. As he was doing this I began to cool down.

'Where do you live?' he asked.

I answered.

He ordered the fierce-looking soldier to search me. 'Everywhere,' he stressed, in Hebrew. 'Thoroughly.'

I was taken behind the curtain. Usually my status as a lawyer spared me from this. I could have refused to be searched. I could have said that I was a lawyer and I had the books and files to prove it, that it was not appropriate for a lawyer to be searched every time he entered the building. But I decided it was not worth it. I wanted to go in and finish the cases that had been pending for two years because the officer in charge of legal affairs had been on military service.

Despite the orders of the young soldier I was given only a cursory search, which I endured with some dignity. I was wearing my coat with the velvet collar, a jacket and tie, an astrakhan hat and a burgundy cashmere scarf. I stood straight, spread my arms and gave the soldier the opportunity to do his job.

I returned to the counter. The young soldier was still looking through the book. A man carrying files entered, spoke some words in Hebrew and left the gatehouse. He had obviously not been asked for his identity card. The older soldier had thought that the rules applied to everyone and asked his younger colleague why this man was an exception.

'Jews don't need passes,' the young soldier explained, stressing the word Jews.

I pretended that I did not understand Hebrew. I had insisted on speaking Arabic.

The young soldier had now flipped through all the pages of his book. He wrote down my details and gave me a pass. All this waiting, this anxiety, this emotion, this humiliation just to get to the officer, Jean Claude, a French Jew who was going to hear nothing more than an objection to the registration of a trademark for a deodorant.

I saw more uniformed soldiers than usual as I walked from the gatehouse through the wooded grounds leading to the main building. Who knows which of these people had shot and killed or maimed a fellow Palestinian? They are criminals, I kept reminding myself; I am walking among criminals. I remained calm, collected. Before coming here, I had told myself that I would do my work as necessary. I would smile at no one, remain distant and aloof.

When I entered his office, Jean Claude seemed so pleased to see me. I shook his hand but did not return his smile. Despite the great warmth in his office I decided to keep my coat and jacket on. This way I would be as formal as possible. After I finished my work I proceeded without delay to Al-Haq for our weekly Wednesday meeting.

In Ramallah, as in other towns and villages, the soldiers were manning roads and stopping people and cars. If there was a stone barricade blocking traffic or graffiti painted on a wall, they would order passengers to remove the stones and paint over the graffiti. One morning I left the house in a rush for an interview with the Christian Science Monitor at the Al-Haq office. When I arrived, I remembered that I had left my heater on so I asked the driver who had brought me to drive me back.

At the corner, just near the mayor's house, we encountered soldiers. I had wanted the driver to take the turn before, but he had wisely refused. The soldiers would have suspected we were trying to avoid them, that we had something to hide.

A soldier told us to stop and get out of the car. 'Now give me your IDs,' one of them said – all this in a businesslike, matter-of-fact way.

After we did as we were told, we were ordered to go and pick up the stones.

I refused.

'You don't want to pick up the stones?'

'No.'

The soldier called his commander, who promptly came over. To explain our behaviour, the driver said, 'If we pick them up the boys will hit us.'

'Then you don't care about your IDs?' the soldier asked.

I stood my ground. Another soldier approached me with his baton raised threateningly. I recalled what the veteran proponent of non-violent resistance Mubarak Awad had told soldiers when they had threatened to hit him: 'You want to hit me. Go ahead.' I wasn't sure I could do the same.

I could see no easy way out of this. I was certain

the soldiers would hit me. I looked at their faces – young, in their early twenties. One had a small, round face and ginger hair. The other, the commander, had a darker complexion and an untrustworthy look. Neither looked cruel. I observed them without any great emotion.

'I am a lawyer,' I said. 'I know the law doesn't require me to pick up stones from a barricade erected by other people.'

I didn't believe this would have any effect, but since I was going to be hit anyway I said it for the record. I produced my lawyer's card. My hands were trembling. The soldier with the baton looked at it and backed down. They conferred among themselves. 'This seems to be an important man,' I heard one of them say. They returned our documents and we drove off.

Further up the street we saw a young man picking up the stones. He was almost finished. This was why they hadn't insisted. There were enough for the one man already there. They didn't need us – certainly not if we were going to be difficult.

What was interesting to me was that before this incident I had mistrusted myself. I thought I would be unable to control my anger and I would do something stupid. That was why I had, until then, avoided confrontation. I stayed home or took alternative routes or avoided making eye contact with soldiers. Now I trusted my ability to stay in control. Yet I still sometimes felt afraid, and fear works in mysterious ways. It was not so much fear of arrest or being brutalised that worried me. It was the fear of losing myself.

The first time I met Henry after the start of the intifada was in early March 1988 in Jerusalem, at the home of my friend Judy Blanc, a Jew originally from New York and one of a generation who had left their country to come to Israel. I had last seen Henry in the June before the intifada. I had agonised about meeting him, but once we met in her bright and cosy kitchen I realised I still cared for him, as one child cares for another, without thinking why. During the past few years we had communicated over the phone and written to each other but had met only sporadically.

In Dostoevsky's *The Idiot*, Parfion Rogozhin tells Prince Myshkin, 'When you're not in front of me I start hating you at once. Over these three months when I haven't seen you I've hated you every minute, honest to God. I felt like poisoning you. That's how it was. Now you haven't been with me a quarter of an hour and all my anger passes off, you're as dear to me as ever you were.' I felt the same towards Henry.

But once back in the loneliness of my house, I couldn't forgive Henry for coming to Israel. He had reaffirmed the Zionist dream by doing so. Here was an educated Jew, with a doctorate from Yale, with good prospects for a career in the West, and he had left everything to settle in Israel and start a family here. His move, his happiness here, suggested to others that if they came they too would be happy.

At Judy's Henry and I spoke about *sumoud* and how it had been replaced by other forms of civil resistance – commercial strikes, stone-throwing, mass demonstrations and refusal to cooperate with the military government administering the Occupied Territories – all intended to indicate that the population was fed up with the occupation and would do everything necessary to bring it to an end. We spoke of nothing else, nothing of my recent thoughts about him. Perhaps we would remain friends – friends from two very different worlds, rarely getting together but often on each other's minds.

Later that afternoon I listened to Dvořák's *New World Symphony*. I remembered how I had cried as I listened to it on my Walkman on a plane to Geneva, where I had gone to do human rights work. I cried because the music made me feel the weight of oppression. It was free and yet I wasn't.

It was nearly Easter 1988. My friend and future wife, Penny Johnson, and I were looking forward to a performance of Bach's *St John's Passion* at the Church of the Redeemer in Jerusalem and to spending the night there and waking up in the morning to the chiming of bells.

'Why are you staying overnight?' my mother asked. 'Will it be a long concert?'

'Yes,' I said, 'and it's safer to spend the night in Jerusalem than return late at night.'

Before we left Ramallah, I saw my neighbour in her garden. Her two sons, George and Issa, were helping her, though the handsome Issa, with a lock of hair hanging over his brow, seemed mostly to be standing by. When I asked what she was planting, she said tomatoes and peppers. In 1967, she added, her sister had planted eight tomato seedlings. They'd produced enough to feed two families and she sun-dried what was left for use later in winter. Meanwhile, her sons had invested $5,000 in setting up a new pizzeria. Two days after it opened the intifada erupted. Four months later they had to close their restaurant because the leaders of the intifada insisted – as part of the civil disobedience campaign – that the town close down at eleven every morning.

On our way to the Old City we stopped at the American Colony Hotel, where we met a journalist who told us that the Israeli army was going to make an announcement at six that evening. Just an hour later we heard that the Gaza Strip had been sealed off and was under curfew for three days, that telephone lines to Gaza had been cut and that journalists were not allowed to travel there except with a military convoy. The West Bank would also be sealed off from Israel for three days. I wondered how that was possible. The land was one.

We immediately realised that we could not stay overnight in the Old City. We feared that, if we did, we might not be allowed back to Ramallah. The thought occurred to me that perhaps it might be good to be in Jerusalem, where I would be able to contact the outside world should I need to. But then I dismissed the idea. I had to get home.

We left the car in the American Colony Hotel car park and entered the Old City through the Damascus Gate. The alleyways, lit by faint yellow street lights, were empty except for the occasional unit of eight soldiers lying down on a large piece of cardboard like squatters.

The concert was at eight thirty. It was still only five past seven when we arrived at the Lutheran Hostel, where we had booked a room for the night. On the way to the hostel we passed a row of new stone houses built for Israeli Jews. Next to them was an Arab house. A woman looked out of a window on the second floor and called for her son. Was there fear in her voice or was it my imagination?

How could the Israelis have expected us to take this lying down? To allow them to come and take our property even as the media reported it all? What of law, what of morality, what of common decency? I said this to Penny, but she did not respond. She was nervous.

After a quick dinner, we went to the Church of the Redeemer where the pastor had reserved two excellent seats for us. 'I'm going to enjoy this,' I told myself. 'Let the music go through me, overwhelm me, relax me, make me forget the trials that are to come.'

I was not disappointed. We stayed to hear Peter's denial of Christ and Christ's suffering as he was taken. We left before the trial and the crucifixion.

We walked through the dark, empty streets. We talked to keep up our spirits, but we were both on edge. We remembered the stories we had heard of how soldiers stopped people, any young men they could find, and beat them up.

This war was different from other wars. This wasn't a war between armies following the rules of engagement. This was a war between combatants and civilians. To the Israelis we were all potential terrorists against whom the worst behaviour was justified.

At the American Colony Hotel we looked for our friend Rita Giacaman, a professor of public health at Birzeit University. We had planned to meet her there and return together to Ramallah, but we couldn't find her. Penny went to look for her.

I sat waiting. Clearly the Israelis were following the recommendations of their American supporters, who advised them to close off the Occupied Territories and do what they had to do – ruthlessly, quickly and without observation by journalists. I was offered a Cointreau and, as I drank it, I couldn't take my mind off what we were returning to. It seemed as though everything we did and said was for the last time – before we vanished deep inside a dark hole, never to re-emerge.

Penny eventually found Rita and Rita, who was chain-smoking, spoke even faster than usual and was anxious that we did not linger. As we were leaving, we met the film-maker Michel Kleifeh, who had just returned from Gaza. 'You can cut the tension there with a knife,' he said. 'It is terrible, terrible down there.'

The road to Ramallah was empty, except for several army jeeps. It felt like a war zone, yet we were not even stopped. On the radio was the news that Gaza had been completely shut down as of ten o'clock.

Next day at Al-Haq we discussed what we could do, how we would work under these new restrictions and what we would do if the telephone lines were cut as in Gaza. No one had an answer.

The closure applied only to Palestinians, not to Israeli settlers, who could still come and go as they pleased and terrorise the population. Many settlers used Tireh Road, where I lived. One day they stopped the mayor's son, his wife and his child in their car. They pointed their guns at him, intending to kill him, but the baby began to cry. The settlers said they would have killed him if it hadn't been for the child.

Every week the Unified National Leadership of the Uprising, a group of underground leaders representing the various Palestinian political factions, issued a bulletin that indicated the form of non-violent resistance that should take place each day of that week. The 22 March bulletin said that 30 March, Land Day, would be a day of protest followed by two days of planting tomatoes, chickpeas, broad beans and spring onions. On the other days of that week the town would open for only a few hours in the morning.

The morning after the bulletin was distributed the army came and closed the vegetable market. They turned over boxes of vegetables and threw the dough at the bakery on the ground. They then tried to force the shopkeepers to open their shops, but the whole town remained closed in solidarity.

The Israelis wanted to be sure that Land Day passed without protest. This was important to them because the US secretary of state, George Shultz, was coming and the government wanted to show him that the area was under control. A massive number of Israeli soldiers were deployed as a result, even as Israel suffered great financial losses by preventing 150,000

Palestinian labourers from working in Israel. During that week every single Palestinian in the street was stopped and had his or her identity card confiscated. The soldiers had orders to be as strict and brutal as possible.

Almost a year later, on 14 February 1989, I received a poem from Henry:

I miss you. I miss our friendship:
I want to reach out across the chaos, the abyss
But so often I feel there is too much blood which
Separates us; too many bullets, deaths and hates
That we cannot be walking the hills, with a distant
View of the Jaffa you never knew as a child
But we are as we prophesied consumed by our
Collective identities, you Palestinian, me Israeli,
You no longer submissive, me, brutalising, brutalised;
You victim, sacrifice; me murderer, worse.

And yet, and yet, all this comes at a time when
Trickster-like, peace, change, transformation is now more
*   than ever a possible reality, a dove to be*
Stroked and cuddled, nested and brooded; in the
Long run, there is much to be hopeful about
If the PLO has recognised Israel, then surely even Israel can
*   and will (alas in her sad slow time)*
Do the same; and so for once a mutuality
And shoulder-to-shoulder work of reconciliation
Together-apart.

The vision is there but like the punishment of Tantalus
It disappears only when we reach for it.
But less strife shall come, and who knows even
For a time, hopefully for a long time, a peace will come.
Yes, the hate, the misgivings, the pull and take
Will simmer ready to rouse to the fuse
But
But for now, it is horror, murder, infanticide
Become banal.
And we Jews on the Israel side who strive for peace
We make acts and gestures but we are not yet committed
Enough, to bring the change we need to share Palestinian
Fate, to be brutalised, checked, jailed and more
To leave off the luxury which we have of attending
To their cares, but stay stuck to this goal
Of opposing oppression, even in God's name.

So what I want to say to you,
My eyes are filled with tears
I am still your friend
If you or your condition will allow.

Upon receiving this letter, I felt that I too missed him, yet our friendship was a luxury I could not afford. Despite his words, I was not sure he really understood the full impact of Israel's policies and the suffering they were causing us. Words were not enough. Tears were not enough. It was action that was needed now. Everyone, Israeli and Palestinian, had to do their part to fight the injustice and I was not sure that Henry had yet understood this.

The Bougainvillea

We arranged to meet at the American Colony Hotel in Jerusalem. As usual, any ill-feeling I had towards Henry melted away when I saw him. We sat in the cellar bar with our drinks and talked. And I left feeling well disposed towards him. But after that, with the more frequent closure of Ramallah, our meetings became sporadic. It was harder for me to get to Jerusalem and with Henry's beard he would be taken for a settler, which would make it unsafe for him to be in Ramallah.

On the Jewish New Year, 14 September 1989, Henry sent me another letter:

I wish I could write you words of hope but in the short run there will be more horror, more blood, more dead. As I said at our last meeting at the American Colony, I have tried to express my feelings in more active ways. I am now an active member of four anti-occupation organisations. 21st year, which I urged to protest house demolitions as illegal, immoral collective punishment, and for which a group was arrested. A religious peace group, Netivot Shalom-Oz Veshalom, which does symbolic vigils and actions to stir the repressed Israeli moral sensibilities. Imut, a group of psychologists, mental health workers who, alas, true to their trade, are more committed to talk than action. And one ad-hoc anthropology protest group concerned with cultural issues and oppression. I have been on condolence visits, e.g. to the village of Nachaleen, and for at least five months met regularly with a small group of Palestinians in Ramallah on dialogue and helping each other achieve

a real political change and alleviation of suffering. So
in a way I am more active and I refuse to lose hope that
peace, reconciliation, fellowship is possible despite all
to the contrary. I have been writing about Abraham as a
model of a peacemaker and I will send you that soon. It
is important in Israel to show how my namesake, Enoch,
related to the land and its native inhabitants in a way
so different from today's fanatics and with moral vigor
unmatched.

At the end of his message he wrote:

Did you not teach me that life is like a cucumber,
sometimes in your mouth sometimes in your ass? Oh
God, let there be a stop to all that – must stop – and a
new year of justice, peace and more.

Yours,
Henry

PS The Israeli army finally caught up with me and I wrote
that I was a pacifist and would not learn to bear arms
and kill and miraculously I was given a deferment!

The letter left me cold, even though what I'd told
him seemed to have had an impact. It seemed too little
too late.

7

An Interlude

Jerusalem, 1980

Perhaps I was slow, but it took me more than a decade after the start of the Israeli occupation to realise that it was not going to end any time soon. The Israelis, I understood, were here to stay and we would have to live with them. I decided I should learn their language so that I could communicate with them and practise law in the Israeli courts, where the work would be more challenging and professionally more satisfying than in the West Bank. On that point, I was mistaken. Israeli military courts were a parody of real courts. Israeli officials used their legal expertise to devise ways of justifying the theft of our land.

Many Palestinians, however, would not learn Hebrew. I recall a professor at Birzeit University who made no effort to study the language and was frustrated when Leumi, the Israeli bank, refused to send him statements in Arabic. 'They make me feel like a complete illiterate,' he complained to me angrily. 'I sent a stiff letter to the manager of the bank and threatened to withdraw my money if they didn't, but nothing came of it.' Half a century of occupation and despite its large number of Arab customers Leumi continues to avoid using a single word of Arabic in any of their statements and letters.

I should have understood that Israel did not seek to cultivate neighbourly relations with the Palestinians, nor did it have a vision of future peace and coexistence. Instead, it was looking for ways to encourage the Palestinians to leave. The fact that the military government, which was responsible for education in the West Bank and Gaza, did not introduce Hebrew into the school curriculum should have been a strong hint.

In Mandatory Palestine my father used to talk with his Jewish colleagues in English, which was also the language of the higher courts. But when he tried to do the same with Israeli officials after 1967 they responded in Hebrew, defiantly, as though to assert that they were Israelis, this was Israel not the British Mandate, and Arabs were now under their jurisdiction and must speak their language.

For four and a half months in 1980 I crossed every day into Jerusalem to attend all-day Hebrew classes at an *ulpan*, a school for the intensive study of Hebrew designed to teach adult immigrants to Israel basic conversation, writing and comprehension skills. I knew about the revival of the ancient biblical language as a language of daily use, but I was still surprised at its success. All Israelis, young and old, recent immigrants or long-time residents, spoke the new language, albeit with a variety of accents.

In one of our discussions about Israel Henry had said that the revival of the language was perhaps Zionism's greatest achievement. Having a common language was indeed vital to the creation of the new Israeli nation. When I attended classical music concerts at Beniani Haoma in the Jewish quarter of Jerusalem, I never ceased to be impressed listening to the old ladies, who were the majority of the audience and who had evidently been born and raised in Germany, Poland or some other European country, conversing in Hebrew rather than in their native tongue. Hebrew had replaced their first language, just as they had exchanged the names their parents had given them for Hebrew names. They had tried to become fully Israeli.

The Israeli linguists worked hard. They managed to find Hebrew equivalents for musical terms and for different kinds of food, plants and flowers. Yet when it came to the Nakba, there was no word for it in Hebrew. The media and officials chose to use the Arabic word instead. It was the same with intifada, or uprising, which was deemed to sound more threatening in Arabic than its Hebrew equivalent, *hitna'arut*. Likewise ceasefire, *tahdi'a*, for agreements instigated by the Palestinians. The Hebrew, *hafsakat esh*, which came to sound more trustworthy, was reserved to designate ceasefires declared by the Israeli army.

Except for one other Palestinian, a young engineer working for the Jerusalem municipality, all the other students in my class were Jews who had come to Israel from a variety of countries, including Australia, Iran, the United States and Uzbekistan. In my class there was an attractive woman from Australia who had short black hair, intense intelligent eyes and a curious, active mind. She and I often conversed during the *hafsaka*, the fifteen-minute break. When I asked her why she had come with her husband from Australia she told me that she had been sickened by the rampant anti-Semitism there. But now what disturbed her here was the orthodoxy she encountered in Jerusalem.

'You ask them why this is forbidden and why that,' she said. 'You genuinely want to know. They always answer you by saying, "*Kakh katov*" [so it is written]. And this is supposed to end all discussion. It's intolerable.'

Our teacher was in her early forties, stout and maternal with a deep voice and an impressive fifteen years' experience at teaching the language. She had been born in Palestine at the time of the British Mandate and her father had studied at the American University in Beirut, where I'd studied. She was able to pronounce the strong guttural sounds that Hebrew shares with Arabic and yet she taught the language with a European pronunciation. I found this strange. It meant that I learned to pronounce Hebrew like an Ashkenazi, though at that point I was unaware of what this signified.

On the first day of class, before the *hafsaka*, I was told that the teacher wanted to see me. She was keen to make sure that I knew I was welcome in her class. She told me she had taught Arab students before (she didn't say Palestinian) and that Arabic speakers found Hebrew much easier to learn than most of the other students. She told me, not without pride, of her star pupil, Ziad Abu Zayyad, who was the very best student she had ever had and who now works as a translator from Hebrew to Arabic. She was as good a guide as anyone could have, having seen thousands of students embark on a new life in this country. The message she wanted to pass on to me was that I should not be impatient with the others and should not act as the star of the class. She wanted to make me feel welcome but remind me that teaching Palestinians was not her priority.

From that very first day I was impressed with how she handled the class, insisting that everyone speak only Hebrew. It was a stressful job, having to teach such a motley crew from different countries and with different abilities. I later learned that she had a wooden frame like a stretcher at home on which she wove floor mats using a large needle and thick woollen threads. This was what she did for relaxation, digging the thick long needle in and out to thread in the colours.

Besides teaching Hebrew, the *ulpan* offered insight into how people from countries east and west were socialised and absorbed into Israel. The school had a number of Jewish-American students who came here in their summer holiday to learn not only the language but also about Israeli 'folklore' and to hear lectures to encourage them to 'return'.

We learned the classic Hebrew songs. At first I would find myself singing along, until I learned enough of the language to understand that these were songs sung by the early Jewish settlers about the joy of settling the land. Then I stopped and just listened to these young people from around the world joining together in propaganda songs in a new language that they were keen to acquire so they could partake in a new life here.

Every few weeks the class would be visited by a short, energetic man with a large yarmulke that covered most of his head and a proud bushy moustache. He would proceed to play Israeli folk music on his accordion and invite us to stand and stamp our feet to the beat, singing, 'Come what may, we will stay and continue our yearning for peace.' Then, having stirred up the class, he would nod to the teacher and walk away, still playing his instrument, leaving us to calm down and return to our less rowdy studies.

Often the teacher would introduce some history into the classes. She would describe how Israel was established, how the land was mainly empty of people, and how the Jewish immigrants came back to develop their ancestral home and make it prosper. As she spoke I would become increasingly angry. One day I could take it no longer and asked to speak. She gave me the floor. Addressing the teacher, I asked how she could describe Palestine as having been mainly uninhabited when she grew up here. She must have realised there was a thriving Palestinian nation living here, most of whom were forced out in 1948. As I spoke in my shaky rudimentary Hebrew, an embarrassed silence fell on the classroom. When I had finished, the teacher smiled and, without comment on what I had said, she praised me, with evident pride: 'Do you realise that you have been speaking Hebrew for the past five minutes?' She was a good Hebrew teacher.

Many years later a number of the residents of the old Arab quarter of Hebron decided to learn Hebrew. Their mixed class of men and women was featured on Israeli TV. Asked by the Israeli reporter why they were studying Hebrew, they answered that it was in order to understand the orders the soldiers bellowed at them and avoid getting into trouble or being shot. A few added that they believed the Jews were going to be in their city for a while so they had better learn their language to communicate with them.

They were taken to the narrow streets outside the classroom, where their relaxed and confident young Palestinian teacher began pointing out various signs in Hebrew and asking them to read them. These were the new names that the Jewish settlers had given to the Arab quarter of the old city. They came upon some writing on the wall and the teacher asked if they could read it. They couldn't.

So he began: 'What is this first letter?'

'M.'

'And the second?'

'A.'

Then he read it for them: '*Mavet la aravim*. You know what this means? "Death to the Arabs."'

8

Allenby Bridge

1992

Penny and I were returning to Ramallah from Washington with the Palestinian Delegation, tired and despondent after a year of futile negotiations with the Israeli delegation that had begun with such high expectations the year before. The Madrid Peace Conference of 1991 had brought together representatives from Israel, Jordan, Lebanon, Syria and the Palestinians, and it had been followed by bilateral negotiations between Israel and a joint Jordanian-Palestinian delegation in Washington. What we could not know, and would not learn until 1993, was that secret negotiations taking place in Oslo between Israel and the PLO would succeed in reaching an agreement between the two sides.

On the Jordanian side of the Allenby Bridge, which crosses the River Jordan, we had completed all the formalities and were waiting for the Israeli soldiers to give us the signal to drive across the border when a sprightly young Jordanian soldier leaped on to the lower step of the minibus. All we could see was his head. He had short-cropped hair and a thick moustache.

'Are these the Israeli soldiers?' he asked, indicating two soldiers on the Israeli side of the border. They had long, dishevelled hair and walked with heavy steps. They seemed self-absorbed, drained by the oppressive summer heat.

'Are these their soldiers?' he repeated. 'These? I could squeeze a dozen of them with my bare hands.'

He turned to us and winked. He had a self-satisfied, superior smile on his face, his eyes dark and triumphant. Then, leaping down from the bus and waving to us, he said, '*Assalam alaikum* [Peace be unto you].'

The soldiers who gave us the order to proceed disappeared and we rumbled over the old, wobbly bridge, underneath us the loose planks of wood supported by the metal edifice that stretched over one of the most troubled waterways in the world. We were on our way home.

Khalid, whose puffy cheeks looked as though they had been inflated with an air pump, alighted from the bus first and the rest of us followed. We were accompanied by a Jordanian porter, who had piled our luggage on a carrier. He pulled it to where there was a yellow metal gate just beyond the bridge and stopped. We could not go any further until the Israeli soldiers came to meet us. We waited but no one came. I leaned over the railing and looked down at the Jordan.

I remember seeing a photograph taken about a hundred years ago of a man rowing his boat along this same river. It had been so much wider then and the branches of the eucalyptus trees along its bank hung over the water. Ever since I had seen this photograph I had yearned to one day row my boat here after the mines had been cleared and the barbed wire removed and the river returned to what it used to be used for – irrigation for farmers, pleasure for visitors and a means of replenishing the dwindling waters of the Dead Sea. But with the negotiations between the Israelis and the Palestinians as they were, this seemed unlikely.

Still no Israeli soldier came to escort us. Uncharacteristically, the bridge seemed deserted. Eventually, a Palestinian porter working for the Israelis walked over to pick up our luggage and the Jordanian porter went back. Khalid was still looking for someone to talk to, someone in uniform, but no one came.

How easy it is for things to be stripped of their significance and their emotional associations. A small yellow gate on the bridge was just a gate, a nearby observation post just a shabby little cabin, the River Jordan just another river.

On the Israeli side of the border we sat on a bench underneath a eucalyptus tree, where we waited like tourists or picnickers by the side of the river, enjoying the shade in the lowest place on earth. Finally, an Israeli soldier appeared. He was light-skinned and red-haired, with what looked like a two-day-old beard and a large, blue-rimmed yarmulke on his head. He was, of course, carrying his machine gun. He asked us in his poor English for our permits.

'You are not important people,' he said, examining them.

'No,' I answered. 'Not particularly.'

He caught the cynicism in my voice and explained, 'You don't have an Aram [the Israeli permit issued for Palestinian VIPs].'

'No,' Khalid said, 'we don't have an Aram. We are members of the Palestinian delegation to peace talks with your country. We don't need one to cross.'

The point was lost on the soldier. It appeared that he had not heard of the delegation or the negotiations. He insisted, 'But you don't have the Aram.'

'No,' Khalid repeated, his face turning a pomegranate red, 'we don't. As I said, we are members of the Palestinian delegation. We have special status.'

The soldier turned to Penny. He must have wondered what a blonde woman was doing with the Palestinian delegation. He asked her, 'Do you have a Palestinian passport?' He no doubt meant the identity cards issued to Palestinians by the Israeli authorities.

Penny smiled and said, 'No. Not yet.'

We were escorted to the customs area, where we met an Israeli official in an orange uniform. She wanted to search our briefcases. We refused because they contained our negotiation documents, which included sensitive information. She did not understand why she couldn't search our bags as she did everyone else's. It fell on Dr Mamdouh Aker, another member of the delegation, to explain in his quiet and patient manner that we were members of the *Wafd*, the delegation.

'It's Friday,' the soldier muttered as Mamdouh gently extracted his bag from her hands. What was one more bag to search on that hot, dry day in

August? She did not care who the owner of the bag was, whether he was a member of a peace delegation. She just wanted to go home to begin her Sabbath. She probably couldn't differentiate between the people across the counter from her. All Arabs looked more or less the same to her.

She waited. I turned to look at the people lined up behind us, waiting patiently. We were holding up the queue. What did they think of us – the self-important suit-clad men and women with our 'James Bond cases', as the bridge security man had jokingly described our bags? Did they make allowances because of the nature of our mission? I doubted it. From the way it looked, they seemed only to resent us for taking up too much time.

Our bags were taken to be X-rayed. Soon it became apparent that this was our punishment. The other passengers were going through customs, but we were kept waiting. In the hope of getting a reprieve, I went with the kind doctor to look for the bridge commander. We asked a young soldier for his whereabouts. Without saying anything to us, he raised his walkie-talkie to his mouth and called his superior. We stood in silence. Then, to break the silence, I asked, 'If we can't work out something as minor as this, how can we make peace together?'

The young man did not respond. It was as though he was enclosed in a thick glass case. I was unable to make an impact, unable even to hurt his feelings. My attempts to communicate or even to insult him left hardly a mark.

The bridge commander finally showed up. He was a

short man with a round head and large black eyes. He was accompanied by a customs officer.

'What are your orders regarding the members of our delegation?' Mamdouh asked the commander.

'No orders,' he answered quickly. 'We just work things out.'

'What does "work things out" mean?' I asked. 'You must have received specific orders and I have the right to know what they are, to know where we stand.'

The commander had said all he was prepared to say, but the customs officer, looking at me kindly, said, 'Respect, to treat you with respect.'

I don't know why this got to me, but I immediately snapped, 'You should know that we don't get respect from you.'

I turned to the commander and continued, 'I want you to know that we don't ask for privileges. We just want to know where we stand.'

'It will be all right,' the commander said to placate me. 'We just want to look very briefly into your bags to see if there is anything for customs. That's all.'

Now I understood. The Israelis were not interested in reading or copying our documents. They didn't take the negotiations in Washington seriously enough. In any case, when they needed to know what we were working towards, they had enough informers to supply them with any intelligence they needed. They did not need our documents. Instead, they just assumed that because we were Arab we would do anything to smuggle goods across the border without having to pay duties.

The search was superficial. No one paid any attention to the documents. It was over very quickly. We were moving to the next station when the customs officer said to me, 'Now we can be friends.' He stretched his hand to me.

I shrugged my shoulders and moved away.

'That's making peace? That's the respect you show?' he asked.

I turned back and stood before him, intending to be cold and unrepentant. But seeing him made me aware that he was a Middle Easterner like me. Judging from his accent, he probably came from Iraq. I could see that he was genuinely hurt by my remoteness. I was sorry – but too proud to admit it.

Later, after the peace accord between Israel and the PLO had been signed, I travelled to Amman to visit my sisters. I had heard how tenacious the Palestinian team had been in negotiating Palestinian sovereignty and claiming the Allenby Bridge as a Palestinian, not an Israeli, border. Palestinians were so proud of this symbolic victory, but my experience at the bridge made me aware how meaningless, how vacuous, it was.

To cross the border, I gave my bag to the Israeli official, who stamped my Israeli permit. Then, passing a Palestinian official in a dark-blue suit standing under a Palestinian flag, I went to the Palestinian Authority booth – 'The Palestinian Authority Welcomes You,' read the sign – where I was searched by an Israeli official. I then went to the Israeli booth to get my

Israeli identity card, which I had deposited there when leaving for Jordan but had to reclaim when returning to the West Bank. Anyone from Gaza and Jericho then had to proceed to the Palestinian Authority official, who stood in front of a peeling painted glass wall. He took my documents and placed them in a drawer. Through the glass, I could make out the Israeli official who opened the drawer, checked the documents and returned them to the drawer and the Palestinian official in front of the glass. There were Israelis everywhere, but as a Palestinian you were not supposed to notice them. You were supposed to see only your fellow countrymen, the 'only' officials in this border entry point to 'your country'.

It was clear that once again the Israelis had succeeded in practising their Talmudic reasoning on us. We said that we were a nation and wanted our own passports. They gave them to us, but nothing else. Palestinian pilgrims to Mecca could now travel to Saudi Arabia on what was called a passport in Arabic and a passport/travel document in English, but the name did not matter. It still bore the same number as the Israeli-issued identity card, which they used to control our movements and our personal freedom. It was still Israel that approved our entry and exit into the Palestinian Territories.

To all intents and purposes, Israel had annexed the West Bank. Ironically, we had our own time zone – like Israel, we changed to summer time, but not until a week after the Israelis did, which caused endless confusion – but we did not control our land. Through its policy of settling its citizens there, who were subject to Israeli law, Israel was treating the Palestinian Territories as their sovereign territory in every way except by name. The Palestinians spent long hours in negotiations insisting that Israeli forces and government withdraw from the West Bank. Finally the Israelis agreed to redeploy from the five main cities, while retaining the right to re-enter these areas when necessary. As for the Israeli military government, it would withdraw but not be abolished.

On the cover of an issue of *El Awdeh* magazine there was a photograph of Yasser Arafat and John Major, then the British prime minister. Standing side by side, the two leaders seemed equal in every way. In the background there was a large photograph of the Dome of the Rock, which gave the impression that the two were standing in front of the symbol of Arab Jerusalem. It appeared that Jerusalem was ours as well. But it was all make-believe. All we had won was symbols.

9

Mad

Ramallah, 1993

Just after the Oslo Accord was signed in September 1993, I received the following card from Henry:

Dear Raja,

I thought that today, with the signing, it might be possible to renew our friendship. I do not know what you think of the agreement, a media fraud or a modest step in the right direction? But in the hopes of a full peace I am happy to send you my book on Abraham, the First Father, who I hope will 'across the generations show us the pathways of peace'.

If you feel you are able I would be honored to hear from you in return,

Henry

I did not send a response. We had not been in touch for over three years and there was much on my mind.

I was going through the most difficult period of my life and had to deal with my disappointment at how our 'war of liberation' had been aborted. Our victory in the courageous intifada had been turned against us, our triumph becoming our shackles. Rather than ending the occupation, the Oslo Accord had allowed Israel to retain its hold over most of our territory, resume building settlements and relieve itself of the responsibility and expense of administering the civil affairs of the Palestinians by transferring these to the newly established Palestinian Authority. The strikes and civil disobedience continued, but we no longer believed that any good could come of them. At the same time, we did not know how to stop. No one had the courage to say, 'It's over. We've been defeated.' If only we could admit defeat we could begin anew. Instead all our defeats were turned into hollow victories. Nothing was learned.

Our towns were now under Palestinian civilian administration. There were victory parades and celebratory gatherings every time Arafat dropped in. The national anthem was played and the president, arriving in his private helicopter, gave a resounding speech even though the enclave was surrounded on all sides by Israeli checkpoints and Jewish settlements. Each town had essentially been made into a Palestinian ghetto within areas controlled and owned by Israeli settlers. Meanwhile, our minister of culture was on Palestinian television boasting of his great achievements and how hundreds, if not thousands, of Palestinians could now exercise their right of return through identity cards issued to all those who were married and had lived here with their spouse for over four years. He failed to mention the fact that the Palestinian passports issued by the Palestinian Authority bore the same number as the Israeli-issued identity cards. By holding on to the population register, any updates – such as registrations of new births or changes in personal status – had to be approved by Israel, which also controlled the borders.

The only thing worse than defeat is the failure to recognise it as defeat and claim it as a victory. The consequence of our defeat was apparent in how we related to Israel and how Israel had begun treating us. This was how I felt whenever I crossed into Jerusalem. Before the Oslo Accord we refused to allow Israeli soldiers to walk all over us. The struggle was collective. Whenever one person was insulted, we all rallied to their defence. Now we just tucked our heads into our shoulders. How could Israelis be expected to respect us Palestinians when they had defeated us so completely?

I had a meeting in Nablus and rather than drive my car I decided to go by bus. It takes a little over an hour to drive to Nablus, but I much preferred to watch the landscape rising and dipping into attractive wadis than concentrate on my driving. Just as the bus was about to leave, a bearded man came on board. He was wearing a grey djellaba with a single breast pocket in which he had put his green identity card and two pens. He was wearing sandals. With him was a woman, presumably his wife, who was completely covered in black, even to the point of wearing black gloves. With them was a light-haired boy, who made me wonder about this couple's ancestors.

As the bus moved off, the radio began to broadcast a sermon. From the sound of it, I assumed it was from a mosque. The man went over to the driver and asked him to raise the volume, which the driver did. The sermon was about how women were blemished and they must hide their shame by wearing a hijab. Not any old hijab, as worn by many women nowadays, but one with very particular specifications, which he began to describe. The dress must be flowing, not tight, so that it did not show the contours of her body. It must not be transparent and must cover all her skin. Otherwise the woman was as good as naked.

He then began to attack those calling for the liberation of women. He quoted at length from Aisha, one of the prophet's wives. He said that when she went to the tomb of Caliph Omar Ibn El Khattab, she could not go in without first covering her head, so ashamed and reverential was she. If Aisha had to cover her head for a man buried in the ground, how then should a woman face a stranger when she goes out? he asked. It sounded, though – from my understanding, at least – that Aisha had gone out without a headdress and only needed to cover up when she arrived at Omar's tomb.

He proceeded to detail the dress code for women when in the house: long, flowing and not too light. She must only leave the house when she needed something her husband could not get for her, presumably tampons. He pointed out how offensive it was to stop at traffic lights when driving and see in the car next to you a driver with his wife beside him. It was this reference to traffic lights that made me suspect that the source of the sermon was Israel, since we had no traffic lights in the West Bank.

When the bus driver stopped at the petrol station, he turned the radio off. Then, when we continued on our way, someone said, 'Please turn on the cassette.' The source of the sermon was not the radio.

The woman in front of me asked the driver for a copy of the cassette. She wanted to know if she could buy it. She was not wearing a hijab, only a colourful scarf. She had a cute light-haired boy with her who was watching everything with fascination. No, the bus driver said, he couldn't sell her the cassette because it wasn't his. 'It belongs to this man,' he told her, pointing to the man wearing the djellaba.

She asked him if he would sell her the cassette.

'I'm sorry,' he said, 'but it is my only copy and I don't want to give it away.'

The woman appeared sincere. She might have been a researcher interested in the new phenomenon of proselytising through recordings played on public transport. But she also had the sad, strained face of someone who was going through hard times. In the sermon we had heard who was going to be saved and make it to heaven and who would be excluded. Perhaps she was hoping for salvation.

I began to think of the other passengers on the bus. Before the 'peace', it had not been impossible for a person to acquire land to build a decent house, or to buy a car or to live well. In the past, what most people in the bus could afford was what I could afford. But now the gap was growing. Land, and the cost of living, had become expensive. Most of the passengers probably lived at an economic level that denied them so many basic essentials. We had seen economic development, but it had excluded the vast majority of people. This false peace had brought deprivation and economic polarisation in its wake. Many did not have the means to buy what had become newly available at the market or to go to the new restaurants, and it must have hurt. In this context, religion became important. Righteousness would grant you a place in heaven, not those materially better off than you. So went the mantra of the religious fanatic.

We passed the Jalazoun refugee camp. Many of the refugees there had added second and third floors to their houses to meet the demands of the camp's growing population. There were empty plots of land next to the camp, but they were not allowed to expand their camp on to that land. We passed some Palestinian farms, their fields yellow with wheat. We passed hilltop Jewish settlements that were expanding fast. We drove on old roads and bypass roads built for the settlers. We no longer moved along routes of our own making. We had adapted to a new topography.

The world outside Palestine and Israel was trying its best to make the new 'peace' seem real. They didn't care about justice. They just wanted calm – at any price. Among numerous conferences that were taking place all over the world, UNESCO organised a conference in Granada, Spain, called 'Peace – the Day After'.

When I received an invitation, I wanted nothing to do with it. How could there be a day after peace when there was none to begin with? But then a friend who worked for the PLO persuaded me to go. Significant changes were made to the programme and it was to be the occasion when the chairman of the PLO, Yasser Arafat, met the Israeli foreign minister, Shimon Peres, for the first time.

The whole event was carefully framed. UNESCO had lost US support and money because of its policies towards the Third World and its refusal to obey the dictates of the United States. UNESCO director Federico Mayor, who was interested in bringing back the Americans, believed that Israel could be the key and so he did his part in promoting the non-peace and normalising relations between Israel and the Arab world.

To have Israel's presence accepted in the region, it was necessary to gain the consent of several sectors of society. The World Bank had brought around big business; now UNESCO was charged with winning over intellectuals and writers. It drafted an agreement to work with the PLO on joint projects that it could carry out prior to Palestine becoming a member state. The signing of the document would take place under Peres's watchful eye in the Alhambra Palace in Granada, where Muslim–Jewish cooperation had once flourished. Flanking the two leaders as they signed the agreement would be writers, intellectuals and opinion makers from the entire region – from Turkey, Iran,

Egypt, Jordan, Palestine, Morocco, Tunisia and, of course, Israel.

The purpose of the meeting was not, however, as initially declared: for Israelis and Palestinians and various figures from the region to think of programmes for the post-peace culture. It was to give legitimacy to what was happening without any questions being asked. It was all meticulously staged. The participants just had to be quiet and docile.

In the first session I asked how it was possible to speak of peace before even the basic components of peace had been put in place. We Palestinians were still under occupation and the occupiers were pursuing a deliberate policy of settling its own population in the occupied areas. After I spoke, a professor from Tel Aviv University expressed his distress at my inability to look forward. He said that he had been disappointed when he heard me speak about 1967. Palestinians were always speaking of the past; Israelis could also speak of the past, could look back at 3,000 years of history. Another scholar took offence at my use of the term 'occupied areas' because this assumed that there was an occupation, just as there had been in France by the Germans. This, he said, was a lie.

There was more futile discussion, then a tense silence as Shimon Peres entered the hall. He did not utter a single word and stayed for exactly four minutes before leaving to catch a plane. I wondered why he had come at all, but then I realised it was in order to allow the other attendees to say they had met him, along with dignitaries and thinkers from the Arab world.

The meeting was a charade. We were not given the chance to present our ideas for future cultural projects. The objective was purely political.

Among the few writers who refused to come was the Palestinian poet Mahmoud Darwish. In response, the cultural adviser to Shimon Peres had said, 'When Makhmoud [which is how she pronounced his name] Darwish left Israel to join the PLO, I wrote him a letter. Last night I went over the letter and wrote to him this addendum which I want to read to you: where are you, Makhmoud Darwish? Why have you not come to this conference? Now that there is peace and the two sides are getting together, where are you, Makhmoud Darwish?' Her words echoed in my ears long after the event.

The great poet proved to be more astute than all of us in staying away, despite the tremendous pressure that the PLO must have placed on him.

I returned home feeling that I had lost direction. Powerful forces were bringing about quick and unwelcome changes. The question for me was where to go from here, but there seemed to be no like-minded people with whom I could discuss my doubts.

Moving between Jerusalem and Ramallah felt like moving between two utterly different worlds. Coming back to Ramallah, I was struck by the chaos and confusion there. Ramallah was being squeezed out of existence. The flatter lands to the south towards Jerusalem were being taken over by the Palestinian nouveau riche. What was left within the city limits were some hills to the north. They were still beautiful, but rather than being protected, they were now haphazardly scarred by all kinds of tall and ugly buildings that were unsuitable for the steep terrain. Everyone was clamouring for space, yet there was a tacit acceptance that all we had was the land within the city boundaries that the Israeli military government had established prior to the Oslo Accord. Everything outside these limits was not ours and would not be available for the future expansion of the city. That was reserved for Jewish settlements.

The streets of Ramallah were jammed with traffic. At the roundabout in the middle of the city, some tradesmen had parked their cars and draped them with colourful carpets for sale. Everywhere I looked, existing buildings were adding more floors, blocking out the sun. Many new buildings ignored the law that did not permit buildings to be built too close to each other. If they were forced to comply, the owners simply built a structure like an inverted pyramid, with the top floors wider than the lower floors.

How had we come to this?

One day, on the way to Ramallah, I drove through the Jewish settlement of Givat Ze'ev south of the city. I remembered how, during the negotiations leading up to the Oslo Accord, the US State Department was willing to take Israel at its word and believe that they had stopped expanding the settlements. At the time we reported that we had seen with our own eyes that the settlers were building across the road. But the State Department chose not to believe us.

Israeli society was full of itself. It was vibrant, active

and self-assured. Plans were afoot for the celebration of Jerusalem's 3,000-year 'anniversary'. Musicians from around the world were commissioned to produce an opera about King David. The world's finest cultural activities were brought to Israel while we lagged behind without a system, without clarity, without any sense of order. We lived in chaos.

One of the positive consequences of the Oslo Accords was that Israel allowed banks to open in the Palestinian Territories. My law office represented a number of them. One morning I drove to West Jerusalem to meet the Israeli inspector of Palestinian banks at the Bank of Israel to negotiate the terms of their opening.

I was caught off guard. When I used to visit the legal adviser at the Military Headquarters in Beit El for my work, the outside gate put me in the right frame of mind for what was to come. But now I went through West Jerusalem and I could drive to the gate – not park my car and walk up as I did before because I was not allowed to drive to the gatehouse. When I arrived at reception I no longer felt that I was going to meet the apparent enemy. But soon enough, on my first visit there, I was reminded of my status.

When an assistant asked what I would like to drink I only asked for water. The young man obviously resented serving me. When coffee was brought on a tray to the inspector, I tried to be helpful and pass the coffee to him, but he refused to accept it from me. Later he went to get it himself but tripped and spilled it. Serves him right, I thought. The official, originally from some Arab country, then used every means possible to belittle me and make me feel inadequate and uncomfortable, questioning my knowledge of the law and procedure. I looked at him, not sure of how to respond.

It was not easy to adjust to this new form of oppression. What made it worse was that there was so much talk of peace and celebrations even as the gulf between rhetoric and reality grew so wide. It was peace at our expense.

The signing of the peace accords had not brought an end to the human rights violations. Only a few months later the Israeli army killed a Birzeit University student from Gaza who had stabbed a soldier near French Hill in Jerusalem. The police pursued him into the fields by helicopter, where they killed him and left his bleeding body to show on TV. The three border guards responsible were honoured by the minister of police. The one who was interviewed on television was Druze and he described how he had performed this 'heroic deed'. Then they showed the body. Nothing like this used to happen during the intifada. When the soldiers shot a Palestinian they put him in their jeep and drove him immediately to a hospital to get treatment.

Justice was now the prerogative of one side. A short time after a young Israeli lawyer was killed in Gaza, Israeli police announced they had killed his assailants. When a settler was murdered in the West Bank, we were told a few weeks later that justice had been meted out. Justice stood for Israeli power, for retribution.

The message was that Israel was invincible and ready to exact vengeance. Bloodshed, abduction, murder, torture were not beyond the pale. The Palestinians were supposed to believe they could not win. It was futile to even try.

The new attitude to our surroundings started with the roads. I began to wonder how we could continue driving on roads with so many potholes. How did we get to the point of accepting this as part of our every-day reality? When did we resign ourselves to all the obstacles the Israeli army put along our roads and stop insisting on our right of passage. Even the potholes had become politicised. And it still hasn't stopped. Years later, in January 2016, the Arab–Jewish group Ta'ayush were fixing a portion of the road leading to Palestinian villages in the southern West Bank when they were stopped by the Israeli army. They asked why and the soldier answered, 'This is the State of Israel. This route does not need to change. This road needs to remain the way it is. With holes. Because this is the territory of the State of Israel.'

When winter came I also became aware of the discomfort of our rented flat – the many gaps in the window frames, the metal shutters that were difficult to close, the cold draughts. I had thought nothing of it before and enjoyed my life in this flat that Penny and I moved into after we got married in 1988. Now it was as though a veil had been removed and I saw things more starkly, without romanticism, and they appeared unendurable. We were able to withstand so much because we felt a great sense of mission, significance and dedication in our life in pursuit of a cause. Now that it had come to nothing we slumped back to earth with a bang and woke up with all the discomfort of the bruises and the aches from the long and painful fall.

Just after the Oslo Accords were signed, one of the PLO leaders wrote a condescending opinion piece in a local newspaper, *Al Quods*, in which he advised us, residents of the Occupied Territories, to take a rest and leave it to our leadership outside to carry on. But could we? Did we trust them? Had we the confidence that it was right to abandon the fight?

It was distressing to realise that rather than encouraging back leading Palestinian cultural icons, artists and writers like Kamal Boullata, Mourid Barghouti and Samia Halaby – many of whom Israel actually refused to allow to return – Israel was instead allowing thousands of policemen to control us, quelling any dissent to the deal that they had signed with Arafat.

At the entrance to Ramallah was a banner raised above the road that welcomed our leaders, describing them as those who had brought 'honour and glory'. It was painful to have to read this every time I entered the city when all around was evidence of disgrace and humiliation.

I was not in Ramallah when it was 'liberated'. I had planned to be there when the ceremony was originally meant to take place, in January 1996, but perhaps so it could be closer to the anniversary of the founding of Fatah, which was led by Arafat, it was moved to

30 December 1995. I was in the Galilee at the time and so I missed it. This was a great disappointment for me, because I had wanted to be there to see the Israeli soldiers leaving our town. (I seem to have a knack for missing the most important occasions – I often get up to use the toilet while watching a film on television only to return and find I've missed the climax and the best part is over.)

I called my artist friend Vera Tamari, who lived nearby. She had seen it all from her balcony overlooking the street where the police station is. She excitedly told me how, as the soldiers packed up and left, they were pelted with stones.

When Bethlehem was 'liberated' four days before Christmas, I was riding in a shared taxi. The driver had the radio on and it was broadcasting Arafat's speech live from Manger Square. In the car were Palestinian women in headscarves who did not seem to like what was being said and the pride he seemed to be expressing in the Church of Nativity, calling it 'our church in our town'. But how, I wondered, was it ours? We lived among historic religious sites of great significance to a large number of people around the world, but what was our relationship to these places? I knew that this was the birthplace of Christianity and that Palestinian Christians were the original Christians. But what did these places mean to these Muslim women, who probably knew very little about Christianity? It didn't give them a sense of pride, or possessiveness. We took our inheritance for granted. Would this change? I didn't think so.

I was feeling what my father must have felt towards the end of his life, a sense of despair that much of his energy had been expended in a futile endeavour, betrayed by politicians who brought all that he had invested his time and energy into to naught. Could it have been different between our two nations had his appeal for peace been heeded, or were the Israelis determined to proceed on their course? I would like to think that the suffering we had endured could have been avoided.

What was becoming clear was that my *sumoud* was at an end. I was not the only one who felt this way. Many Palestinians were leaving, just as many had left at the beginning of the occupation. In the past the hardships were endurable because there was still hope that our perseverance would eventually bring an end to our suffering. Now, as I faced the incompetence and corruption of the emerging Palestinian administration over civilian life, I began to ask why I should go on with my life in occupied Palestine. Everywhere I went I saw young Palestinians acting as our liberators and glad to return to Palestine carrying guns and wearing army uniforms. How should I deal with this new and perplexing reality? I wondered if it would be best for me to just leave and start a new life elsewhere. I was free to go. I was no longer staying here for a cause.

In the end, what kept me here was my work, my friends and a feeling for the place – all selfish reasons. The hills, in their own way, were replacing politics as a subject of reflection for me. Perhaps it was good that I had the hills as an escape, because in the years after 'the liberation' I was also feeling more lonely than ever.

A number of my Palestinian acquaintances tried to position themselves within the new Palestinian Authority. Ministerial roles were lucrative and available to those who were willing to go along with the authority's policies. I began to detect an unwillingness among some of my friends to criticise the leadership. Was it out of fear, I wondered, or just the politics of expediency? I suspected the answer was both. Many of those who had taken part in the struggle decided it was time to look after their own personal interests. They could not see any advantage to being in opposition. Intellectuals can often be among the most skilled accommodators. They can justify almost anything if they think it is to their benefit. Now, when we talked about politics, these people seemed not to see what to me was obvious, that we were heading towards disaster. They called me a rejectionist and criticised my pessimistic outlook. This inevitably strained our relationship.

Perhaps they had not changed, but the intense collaboration that in the past had produced such closeness was gone. Without the thrill that came from working for a cause greater than ourselves, what remained was lacklustre and opaque.

In my disappointment I had started once again to think of my friends on the other side. I had come to realise how much I missed them. Some, like Naomi, had emigrated to England. But others, like Henry, were still here. I now felt that I should like to renew our friendship.

Just a few days later I went to the Jerusalem Theatre in West Jerusalem to see *The Dance of the Wind*, a dreamy and lyrical Indian film. Afterwards, as I was climbing up the stairs from the basement, where the film was shown, I saw Henry and Iva. I was startled and happy to see Henry. He seemed to materialise on those stairs just as I was ready to resume our friendship. We agreed to meet again.

When I got home I received an email inviting Penny and me to come to his house for tea, but I answered that I would like to meet first, just the two of us, to talk. We met at the Cinematheque café, where we had so often met in the past, and then walked towards the Arab neighbourhood of Silwan, where we sat under a carob tree and talked some more.

I told him that I had missed our friendship and asked him why he thought we had been estranged for so long. He told me it may have been because of my identification with the Palestinian cause and my grief after my father's murder. It had become difficult for me to sustain the friendship when he was not politically involved.

After a pause, he added that he believed I had gone further than my people in coming to terms with Israel and then I had doubled back. 'You went ahead too quickly and could not sustain it,' he said. 'You were angry.'

I did not like this interpretation and told him so. He didn't respond and changed the subject. We drifted from one topic to another, as we used to do when we last met, in 1989. It was as though there had been no ten-year gap in our friendship. I felt genuinely glad to see him, but after we left the café and I was driving back to Ramallah I had a change of heart. We had decided all too quickly not to dwell on our estrangement. Henry had been evasive and unwilling to confront what had made it difficult for us to continue to be friends – his refusal to actively protest against Israel's policies towards Palestinians. It was true that he had written to me reporting that he had taken part in demonstrations, yet in view of the gravity of the situation this had not seemed at all adequate to me.

As I drove I thought further about Henry's explanation for our estrangement, that it was due to my having gone further than my people. Was that Henry being kind and finding an excuse for me rather than blaming me for not staying in touch even when he had tried more than once to renew contact?

But there was more to it. Henry was putting all the blame on me. He had exonerated himself entirely. What did he mean when he said I did not want to see him because I was too angry? It was his way of explaining it all away as a flaw in my character. He had failed to take into consideration what had caused every Palestinian to be justifiably angry.

Back in Ramallah after meeting Henry, I was distracted by everything around me. I found there was something disconcerting about a people that swept the past under the rug and failed to censure the Palestinian leadership for failing its people during its negotiations with Israel. The people, I suppose, were focused on survival. We were experts at this.

Driving around Ramallah, certain buildings began to remind me of this town's grim mysteries. The sight of a house just behind the Amari refugee camp reminded me of a man who was found hanging on a tree in a field in Kufr Akab in 1989, whose case we investigated at Al-Haq. We were never able to discover why he was hanged or who did it. I remembered going to his house in the course of our investigation and finding his dead body lying in the living room, his young wife standing over it in a state of shock. How could it be that he would commit suicide? she asked. And yet who murdered him and why? we at Al-Haq asked, but could not find an answer. If the Israeli army wanted him dead they would shoot him, not hang him from a tree. Could it have been the Israeli settlers? But why him? Was it in revenge for something a Palestinian had done to one of their own?

Further along the road on the right-hand side I saw the flat where a woman had been locked up by her father for some twenty years. She was found by the Israeli army during one of their incidental raids on the building. Her hair was long and unkempt. Her nails were monstrously long. She had not been in contact with any other human being except her father for all that time. She was taken to hospital, but before she could be treated and recover enough to speak, she was murdered. The Israeli police, who had authority over criminal matters, never properly investigated the murder. We never discovered why this young woman was imprisoned for two decades.

I noticed the pharmacy behind Rukab's ice cream

parlour. It was now being run by the son of the pharmacist. One morning several years ago, while the street was busy with shoppers, a masked gunman came into the pharmacy and shot dead his father. The father had been accused of being a collaborator but this was never confirmed. We never knew the outcome of the investigation – or if there had been an investigation at all. These were but a few of the mysteries, on top of my own personal tragedy involving the murder of my father, that had occurred in our small town and remained unresolved.

After that meeting I began to see Henry more frequently and was again pleased with our friendship, taking walks with him and enjoying his company. We didn't mention the break now. It was as if it never happened.

Israel continued to be a country of such complexity. Those like Henry and the other Israelis I had met and befriended over the years were exceptional people, cosmopolitan, experienced, mature, complex … friends. I didn't want to lose their friendship. I felt that my relationships with them had gone through so many phases that they each now rested on solid ground and were in no danger of being trivialised. But this was not how everyone around me felt.

The first and most formidable obstacle that faced anyone trying to think of the new situation was that the Oslo Accords had become political reality. They had entered history and marked a change that could not be willed away. In the past we were not a delusional people. Our strength lay in our ability to dream, to refuse the dismal reality and live as though it would change tomorrow. Otherwise we would have abandoned the struggle long ago. By pretending to be so strong and have so much power and act as though he was a head of state, Arafat played an important role in upholding this dream. But now the Israelis were able to turn it against us through their 'peace'. Perhaps Arafat had such unfounded confidence in himself that, bad as he knew the deal to be, he believed he could eventually turn the tables through the sheer force of his personality. He had to convince his people that it amounted to a victory. He succeeded with most of them, but underestimated how devious and calculating his enemy was. They made sure to block any attempt by the Palestinians at getting out of what they had put their signature to. Our ability to dream was no longer our strength but our weakness, not our uniqueness but our downright madness.

What puzzled me was how ready Palestinians were to exonerate Arafat. It was true he brought visibility to the Palestinian struggle through his leadership of the PLO and had strong control over the organisation. Yet I wondered whether this could also be related to the way our culture treats the father figure, appealing for *rida el lah wa rida el walidayn* (for the favour of Allah and the favour of the parents).

I had always marvelled at how even elderly men from the PLO referred to Arafat as *el Walid* (Father), but had failed to appreciate the significance of this.

In traditional society a father is supposed to know best, so that when he makes a mistake he is not held accountable because he is owed respect, not censure. Surely the father's mistakes were made in good faith, because that was all he is capable of. To many supporters, Arafat was not considered a functionary who could be held to account. His foibles and weaknesses were excused, like a father's.

I've often heard people say of Arafat, 'Poor Father, he sacrificed his life for his people. He's old. He did his best.' I always found this strange. Such an attitude could never be taken by Israelis towards their political leaders. Even the founding father of their state, David Ben-Gurion, was rejected for many years when he erred.

After the deal was signed I took part in a tour of three Scandinavian countries with Haidar Abdel-Shafi, the head of the Palestinian delegation to the Madrid Peace Conference and the Washington negotiations, and Mustafa Barghouti, to explain the pitfalls of the Oslo Accords. When we arrived in Oslo, the Palestinian workers at the hotel where we were staying wanted to meet Haidar. He and I were having a quick lunch when they approached, bearing a gift of fruit. They sat around the old doctor and asked him for his thoughts on and expectations for the future of their country. They were exiles and hoped one day to return to the Palestine that never left their mind. As he peeled an apple with his long, deft fingers, he explained to them about the importance of self-reliance. I knew he was not saying much and that he had little to tell them and no hope to offer, but what he did say he said in a kindly, fatherly manner, his eyebrows curved, his face long and elegant, his fingers continuing to slowly and deliberately peel the apple, which he turned round and round in his hand. They seemed to hang on his every word and be satisfied. But why, I wondered, when he was saying nothing of substance? It was just because he came across as a father figure and that was what they needed.

Afterwards I thought that if I had had to speak on that occasion I would have agonised over what to say to them that could have given them hope. I would have expected to have a programme, a policy, a vision. Otherwise I would not have been able to utter a single word without feeling I was letting them down.

I knew in the depth of my soul that the dignity which comes simply from age in a person like Haidar is its own justification and no other is needed. He was a man who invited respect and acceptance without having to offer anything in return. This privileged state would never be mine. I would never be able to act in a fatherly way towards anyone, as my father could never act in a fatherly way towards me because I never allowed him to.

And so, with my profound feeling of inadequacy, I am doomed to feeling the need to justify my existence through writing and speaking, while assuming the burden of and responsibility for the failure of all I see around me as if it were my own.

After that desperate attempt by Abdel-Shafi, Barghouti and myself to enlighten the Scandinavian countries on which we had so often relied for political salvation, we returned to a melancholy Palestine, where we found most of the public engrossed in their own private concerns, distracted by the money that Western countries were pouring into their divided community in the hope that they could buy the Palestinians' acquiescence and acceptance of their lot, and keep the region under control.

10

Crossings during the Second Intifada

Ramallah, 2000

In September 2000, five years after the Oslo Accords, came a second, more violent intifada. Israel immediately imposed more restrictions on movement and forbade us from using many of the roads. Route 443, a four-lane highway built on land belonging to Palestinian villages, was now reserved for connecting Jerusalem and the Jewish settlements, such as Ramot and Givat Ze'ev, to the coast. Before, we had been able to use it to get to Jerusalem from Ramallah in twenty minutes. Now it was off limits. The highway had always been meant to link the far-flung Jewish settlements to Jerusalem and Tel Aviv. It wasn't for those of us coming from Ramallah, or for those Palestinian villages whose lands had been confiscated to build it.

Henry lived in West Jerusalem, where the municipal government, which was also responsible for East Jerusalem, provided well for all its Jewish residents while neglecting its Palestinian residents. He lived in an attractive, quiet area with parks and clean, well-ordered streets – amenities that our cities could not enjoy after the large-scale confiscation of Palestinian land. I admitted to myself that when I thought of our different living conditions I felt envy, but I put that aside. I didn't want to feel all those strong negative emotions once again, or repeat the recriminations and ruptures of the past. Nor did I want to sacrifice my friendship with him for the cause. I wanted to continue to see him and, despite the difficulties, continue our friendship regardless of where our two peoples stood. Still, going to Jerusalem to see Henry after the start of the second intifada became an ordeal and on the nights before I made the crossing I often dreamed of being stoned on the way. What made our meetings easier was that this time Henry and I were politically on the same side. My heart was not with this armed struggle against Israel, which I saw as futile, but I was still trying to understand and make sense of it all and needed Henry's help.

It was becoming impossible to leave through the Israeli checkpoint at Samiramis, just outside Ramallah, as the road was often closed. So one morning, on my way to see Henry, I followed a procession of cars going uphill in the direction of the Jewish settlement of Psagot. I drove through narrow, winding lanes, on occasion almost passing through people's gardens.

The road through Kufr Akab was closed – by Israel, I thought, as punishment, but I was later told that the Palestinians were having it paved. Eventually, I ended up at the main Israeli checkpoint to Jerusalem.

Fortunately the wait wasn't long. But as I approached Jerusalem I worried that I would not get back to Ramallah on time. Violence usually broke out at Qalandia in the mid-afternoon. If my car wasn't ready by then (I would have it checked while in Jerusalem), I would inevitably have to pass through the battleground. And lo and behold, when I returned to Ramallah I could see young men gathered outside the nearby refugee camp, twirling their slingshots and hurling their rocks at the soldiers. For a moment I thought I heard a rock hit my car, but I was safe.

Earlier, when we met at the American Colony Hotel, Henry talked incessantly about the various books he had just read – mainly novels and books on psychology and religion. He was a voracious reader. He spoke on all sorts of topics, except what I was burning to discuss – what was taking place around us, how to understand it and what to do about it. Henry seemed tense and he would not give me the chance to ask him how he felt. I left feeling exhausted and cheated. It was true I did not want our meetings to be consumed by political discussion, yet the total avoidance of politics and current affairs and how they were affecting our daily lives felt unnatural and forced. So much was left unsaid.

I was on Henry's mailing list for letters that he sent to his various friends around the world. He often wrote about Israelis killed by Palestinian suicide bombers and he could never spare any sympathy for the Palestinian victims or the suffering we have had to endure. Nor did he give any context as to why all this was happening. I wanted to ask him what he thought were the reasons, but he didn't give me the chance.

About a month later I met Henry at his office. It was in an old Arab house with a beautiful tiled floor. He met me at the front porch. The door behind him was adorned with two Israeli flags fluttering in the strong wind. He stood there, short and stocky, his beard seeming longer than ever, framed by the two flags. I had been noticing that more and more religious young men on our side were growing their beards, indicating their support for the Islamic faction Hamas. Why, I wondered, were beards associated with wisdom and religious observance? Was it that so much devotion to God leaves them no time to shave?

Henry had just seen a patient and another was due in a few hours, so he was in a wired and garrulous mood. He was also more evasive than ever. This had caused our rift during the first intifada. Perhaps it was a mistake not to bring up the subject of how he could situate his office in a house that had been taken by force, with no compensation paid to its original owners. Yet somehow we had to conduct our friendship on a plane above and outside politics. How long this would be possible, I didn't know. I supposed it would depend on whether I could remain calm.

In 2002 the Israeli army reinvaded the West Bank and placed us under curfew for most of April and then intermittently until July. Difficult as these four months were, they confirmed to me the importance of my wonderful friends.

Naomi called from England to ask how Penny

and I were managing. Shortly after that, her mother, Rosheen, called from her new home in the Galilee. That brought back memories of the early 1980s, when I worked with Naomi on *The Third Way*. How different those times had been, when we still had hope of peace between Israelis and Palestinians and the countryside was open to us, a place where we could escape when the tension and stress became too much to bear.

Henry and Iva also called, as did my Israeli publisher, Yehuda Meltzer, and his partner, Lily Eiss. They had all become politically involved against the occupation, distributing aid and participating in demonstrations, even though none of these friends had been active in organised politics before. Under the new circumstances, they couldn't hold back. Iva kept saying how ashamed she was, and I wondered why she should be. I condemned the appalling actions of the Palestinians who killed innocent civilians, but it did not make me ashamed of all Palestinians.

On another occasion, I had a long conversation with Iva on the telephone. She told me how shocked she was when she first saw the refugee camps in Gaza, their inhabitants waiting to return even as her parents, themselves refugees, had managed to make a new life for themselves in Israel. She also said her children – her eldest son was thinking of joining the army – did not know about the Nakba of 1948. They were surprised to read about it in my book, *Strangers in the House*. Henry had not told them.

After hearing this from Iva, I imagined what I would say to Henry: *Henry, why didn't you tell them?*

Why did you think it was not important to let them know about me, about us, those who share the land with you? Why did you want to spare them, keep them in the dark? And how, then, did you expect them to become aware and informed, as moral people. Did I and my family tragedy not count for anything to you?

But I could almost hear Henry's response: *What have you done to help? How often did you visit us when the children were growing up? Why did you not come and get to know my children? They could have learned all this directly from you.*

I couldn't plead innocent to the charges.

Two years after the invasion I went to Jerusalem to do a reading at the American Colony Hotel from my book *When the Bulbul Stopped Singing*. I left Ramallah with no difficulty via the eastern exit. I drove through Beitin, which now looked like a military zone and was no longer the pretty farming village it once had been, and then the Qalandia checkpoint, which had started to look like Checkpoint Charlie. East Jerusalem was desolate, empty of people and full of rubbish. I wondered how we had got to this. Whose fault was it? I could find no simple answer. It was not just the fault of Sharon or Arafat or the settlement policy. It was not just religious fanaticism. It was not just the events of the last century in Europe. It was a mix of all of them.

On the way back from my reading, I saw the red signs the Israeli authorities had placed by the checkpoints and at the entrance to Ramallah warning Israelis that it was against Israeli law for them to enter cities and towns under the administration of the Palestinian Authority. These served the purpose of keeping the two sides apart and indicated to Israelis that everywhere else was available for settlements. Who of my Israeli friends, I wondered, would now be willing to break the law and come to visit me in Ramallah? I also saw that some low concrete slabs had been placed in the middle of the Jerusalem–Ramallah road close to Qalandia. Could it be that they were building a wall in the middle of the road, dividing the Arab neighbourhoods that had been annexed to Jerusalem from the other Arab neighbourhoods?

Walls seemed to be going up everywhere, between houses, through hills and valleys, around cities and over roads, making crossings ever more difficult. A former classmate's daughter lived in the area of Al Ram, just north of Jerusalem. A wall now separated her from her mother, who lived in nearby Beit Hanina, which had been annexed to Jerusalem – yet another case of a family divided by a wall since the establishment of the Israeli state.

Even in my worst imaginings I couldn't begin to grasp the full impact of these walls closing in on us. What would become of us? How would we live with walls surrounding our cities and villages? There would be no access to the sea. Only confinement. The fear I felt after the West Bank and Gaza had been sealed off in 1989 would be realised in concrete. I remembered a clip I had seen of the Berlin Wall being built and how menacing it appeared. I felt the same way now.

A few days later I went to have lunch with Henry. He chose Hillel Café in the German Colony, not far from the house where Naomi used to live. A Palestinian suicide bomber had just killed six Israeli Jews and one Palestinian there. I would have preferred a different venue, but Henry insisted. I said it might be dangerous but he said the same place would not be bombed twice. The worst had already happened there.

We ate in the café in silence, but the crime was on both our minds. I thought we would at least mention it, but the moment never came. As we ate, I looked at Henry's sombre face. I could read in his expression a profound sadness and repressed anger. It was so unlike him not to be talkative, but he did not utter a single word.

I tried to imagine how it might have felt for that young Palestinian man to blow himself up, how he had entered this café and what had been going through his mind before he died. I challenged myself to imagine what sort of despair had led to committing such an act, but I couldn't. We finished the meal in silence.

Later Henry told me that he knew two of the victims of the bombing that had taken place there – a medical doctor and his twenty-year-old daughter, who was getting married the next day. Henry's daughter would have been there had it not been for her good fortune. The bomber had tried to go to the pizza restaurant nearby, but it had been well guarded. He arrived at the door here, was stopped, but then set off the explosives. The whole place went up in flames.

I wondered whether Henry had decided to meet me

at this café so that I would be forced to confront the horror. But the only issue he commented on was the practical preventive measures that were later taken to protect the café – as though more security was the answer. He said nothing about the larger, more complex factors, the human and political issues that led these young men to brutally kill themselves and others in despair.

When I got back I tried to imagine the young man with explosives wrapped around his waist walking between the café and the pizzeria, intent on blowing himself up and hurting others, and wrote a short story which I called 'The Man Who Lost His Head'. In the last paragraph I used the exact words of the Israeli proprietor of a café where a similar hideous incident had taken place. This was how I ended it:

> After he was dropped off he took a wrong turn and lost his way. He walked on, anxious and afraid, until he reached a café. It was off the beaten track. Sitting outside, resting on a white plastic chair, was a woman who worked as a waitress. She was smoking a cigarette in the sun. She saw him, a handsome man with large beautiful eyes, and winked at him. He was so surprised by her gesture that he found himself walking toward her. She wasn't like the Israelis he was expecting to find, hateful people who deserved to die. She was a friendly sort, and offered him a cigarette. He badly wanted one, but told himself that he had not come to smoke

with an Israeli. He had given up on pleasure; to live he first had to die. Still, she bid him to come to her. His confusion and vulnerability must have endeared him to her. She was insisting that he come over. The explosive belt around his abdomen made him feel hot. I'm not going to go to her, he thought, but how can I communicate this to her? Running toward her he tore open his shirt, exposing the dynamite sticks. She ran from him screaming, calling for help. He could see that there was someone running toward him. He made a run into the empty café and pulled the string.

That evening the proprietor described what happened:

'My café is in shambles,' he said. 'It was quite a scene. On the only table in the middle of my café that remained standing, the head of the terrorist rested on its side: fair hair smeared with blood, an open mouth, nose, eyes, and one ear.'

Israelis were not the only victims of the shootings and suicide bombings. In one terribly sad incident George, the son of a friend and colleague, Elias Khoury, was killed while jogging near his home in East Jerusalem on 19 March 2004. George was a third-year law student. Someone in a passing car shot and killed him. The Aqsa Brigade later apologised and declared him a martyr. Just imagine the gall, I thought, to kill such a promising young man and then honour him, to act as though they had the power to decide a person's afterlife on God's behalf. It saddened me to think of Elias, who had also lost his father in a bombing at the Mehna Yehuda Market in West Jerusalem in the 1970s. First his father, now his son.

I will never forget the film *Arna's Children* by Juliano Khamis, the son of a Jewish mother, Arna Mer Khamis, and a Palestinian father, Saliba Khamis, which I saw in 2004 in Ramallah. It was about five children from the Jenin refugee camp who all took part in a children's theatre project organised by the director's mother in 1980. A member of the Communist Party at the time, Arna had belonged to Palmach, the underground fighting force of the Haganah under the British Mandate in Palestine, and she didn't regret it. In the film she described the sense of pride and power that came from that association and her work. Her work at the refugee camp was not to prove there were good Jews. It was not to help the Palestinians build their state – she did not believe in nationalism. It was her way of resisting Zionist colonialism. 'The intifada, for us and for our children,' she said, her head completely bald from cancer treatment, 'is a struggle for freedom.'

The film, which was shot over a number of years, followed the lives of some of the children who took leading roles in the Freedom Theatre, a community-based Palestinian theatre located in the Jenin refugee camp. A scene at the beginning of the film showed Arna surrounded by children from the camp. The Israeli army had just demolished one boy's family home and we saw him sitting on the ruins, bristling with anger. Arna encouraged the boy to express his feelings. She told him to hit her, but he couldn't at first. She continued to work with him until he went at her with all his strength, his clenched fists striking her over and over again until he collapsed with exhaustion.

At a later point in the film we saw two of the children, now in their late teens, preparing to engage the Israeli army in a nocturnal gun battle during the second intifada. As the soldiers drove their armoured tanks through the narrow, misty lanes of the camp, the young men armed themselves with guns, improvised explosives and their own untrained ideas of combat.

In a separate incident, one of the children ended up taking a machine gun and firing haphazardly at passers-by in the Israeli town of Khudeira. The immediate cause was the bombing of a school by the Israeli army. He was the first to enter the school, where he saw the dismembered body of a ten-year-old girl. He collected her body parts in his shirt. His friends said that after this he seemed 'to go into himself. He became quiet and religious and kept to himself.' His mother described the last day before the shooting. He asked to take a bath and then asked her to join him for breakfast. He moved around the house looking at it carefully, as though memorising everything there. A friend who was asked what he thought of his actions pointed to the miserable life at the camp. It was like death and, he said, 'if one is going anyway, at least go one's own way with a bang'.

Every member of the group except one was killed by the Israelis. Two died in suicide missions.

Arna's project gave these children a stronger sense of themselves. It lifted them above the rest, giving them ambition and hope. Then came the Israeli invasion of 2002 and they felt a greater sense of responsibility to take action on behalf of others who were not acting for themselves. The camp was not protected by the Palestinian Authority. It fell to them to do something and in the process they sacrificed their lives.

After the film, the director addressed the audience. Juliano, strikingly handsome and talented, told us he had served in the Israeli army as a paratrooper but that he had soon rebelled after he saw the mistreatment of a Palestinian man at a checkpoint. He resented the discrimination and refused to obey an order. As a result he was imprisoned and discharged from the army. He told the Palestinian audience that he felt '100 per cent Palestinian and 100 per cent Jewish', then added, 'The Israeli army is not a congenial place for those like me who feel that way.' But Juliano's rebellion went beyond the rejection of army discipline. His insistence that 'there is no religion, no identity, nothing, we are just human beings' struck at the very heart of a social and political structure in Israel that exploits religion as the basis for determining a human being's place in its hierarchy of privileges and rights. As an artist, Juliano believed that when people of different cultures and backgrounds worked together to create something they were able to overcome the intolerance that isolated them and made them enemies

intent on killing each other. This was why he revived
the Freedom Theatre that his mother had established
in Jenin refugee camp in 1992, when it was called
Stone Theatre. *Arna's Children* was made by a director who knew what anger and hate could lead to and
yet he chose to live and work in Jenin, one of the most
volatile cities in the West Bank. This was because he
recognised the workshops in which he trained young
children to be actors as a solution to the conflict.

I saw the film as a condemnation of our society and
our leadership. I thought that any Palestinian watching
it should be ashamed. There was a discussion afterwards in which several people spoke. None of them
pointed to the tragedy at the centre of the film, that
the defence of Palestinians during the Israeli invasion
was left in the hands of teenagers. Sylvie, a psychologist who joined us watching the film, was the only
person to point this out when, after the discussion,
we met at a café for dinner. She suggested that Arna's
tragedy was that she failed to 'protect' her children. Of
course, by the time they grew up to be fighters she was
dead, but she had started something, lighting a torch,
and certain tragic consequences followed.

For some, Juliano's work was too subversive. There
were those on both sides of the divide who saw a threat
in his 'solution to war' and wanted him gone. Whether
it was for this or some other motive – it never became
clear – one afternoon as he was leaving the Freedom
Theatre a masked gunman emptied seven bullets into
his body, killing him on the spot. It remains unknown
who the killer was. Even though Juliano was an Israeli

citizen, Israel must not have considered him enough of a Jew because, unlike other cases in which a Jew was killed, this heinous crime remained unsolved. Whoever was behind it intended not only to murder Juliano but also to destroy the vision for which he stood.

Just before he died Juliano had directed a superb production of *Death and the Maiden* by the Chilean artist Ariel Dorfman about a victim of torture who meets the man she believes was her torturer. The play was presented at the Qasaba Theatre in Ramallah days after his murder. I was in the audience and Juliano's portrait was projected on to the walls of the theatre where he had often directed plays. The audience was in tears. Juliano was primarily an artist who used the very stuff of his complicated life in his acting and directing, one of the few who crossed borders and embodied in his work and person the ideal of a binational reality. Yet this artist's path was doomed. The divide between Israelis and Palestinians was too wide to be bridged by a single brave heart.

There was a time when it was possible for Jews and Arabs to live together peacefully in Palestine and to intermarry, as Juliano's parents had done. Both groups are Semites and share more similarities than they are now willing to acknowledge. Those who try to cross the line these days have to pay a heavy price.

But there was hope. The murder was not attributed to any Palestinian political faction and it was condemned by most sectors of Palestinian society in the strongest possible terms. One of the tributes took the form of projecting *Arna's Children* on to a large screen in the main square in Ramallah. Numerous symbolic funeral processions took place in most of the major Palestinian cities. It showed how much more favoured Juliano's 'solution to war' was than many believed to be the case.

After the film we went to eat at a new restaurant in Ramallah where we saw two members of the Palestinian cabinet. One of them had written about the 2002 invasion of the West Bank without criticising the Palestinian Authority. Always well dressed and with their assured presence, they would never feel any guilt or, God forbid, responsibility. To feel this you would have had to have an active populace ready to hold you accountable. They didn't – or didn't believe that they did. They were there by virtue of having placed themselves in the higher ranks and they had managed to remain where they were – on top.

At home I wondered who was to blame for the death of the young men in Jenin. Israel and its brutal policies, of course, but also the Palestinian leadership for its failure to lead. If it couldn't assume responsibility for its own people, its failure was criminal.

11

Forbidden Roads*

Jerusalem, 2004

It was April 2004. I was preparing to leave the house to pay a condolence visit to Elias Khoury on the first Greek Orthodox Easter after the death of his son, as is the habit here, but I was feeling anxious. It had become increasingly harder to leave the house. This was another feature of our imprisoned state. We had become too attached to life behind bars. We were afraid that if we left we would not be allowed back. I was becoming like a dear relative for whom every farewell was an ordeal: whenever he came to visit, he had to be forced to leave. Ever since I heard of how my father had left the office that evening before he was murdered, how he had lingered, spoken individually to every-one, started to leave, then returned, I had begun to pay attention to farewells, as though it was necessary to memorise every detail and gesture lest it be the last.

---

*A version of this was published in *Index on Censorship*, Volume 3, 2004.

After the visit to Elias I felt as I usually do when confronted with death. I wanted to live and enjoy life, and so Penny and I decided to continue to Jerusalem and have dinner there.

Whether or not it was prudent to stay late in Jerusalem and risk the return journey to Ramallah through the back roads at night, where several motorists had recently been shot, was questionable. But neither of us was in the mood to be prudent.

We dined and visited friends we had not seen since the West Bank had been sealed off. I was amazed how quickly you can forget about the occupation and all the restrictions Israel had imposed on us, because when I looked at my watch it was already nine thirty. Our respite was over. We had only half an hour to get to the Qalandia checkpoint before it closed. We drove as though demons were pursuing us. When we got there we found two other cars ahead of us. One was allowed through – we didn't know why – while the other was forced to turn back. When our turn came we were apprehensive.

'We live in Ramallah,' I said. 'We want to get back home.'

'I can't let you. It is past ten o'clock. This checkpoint closes at ten.'

I looked at the clock on the dashboard. 'But it isn't ten yet,' I said.

'It is ten forty-nine,' the soldier said.

I remembered that Israel had already changed to summer time. The Arafat-run Palestinian Authority had decided to delay turning forward the clock for no apparent reason except perhaps to distinguish 'Palestine' from Israel.

'But you've just let that car through,' I said.

'Yes, because he had a pregnant woman.'

'It's not a big deal to let us pass. We're tired and we just want to get home.'

But the soldier would not budge and we were not in the mood for pleading or tall stories about sick family members.

'You could go through Surda,' the soldier said, suggesting that we use the back roads.

'But it wouldn't be safe at this hour.'

'For you it would. You're not Israeli,' the soldier said, as though cars in the dark blinked their ethnic origins.

Then I thought of my lawyer's card and presented this to the soldier. He had a pleasant face and was wearing dark glasses even though it was night. He examined it, then looked at me and said, 'But it wouldn't be fair to let you through just because you're a lawyer and not to allow the others now, would it?'

I wasn't sure whether I heard him right. 'Did you say fair?' I asked.

The soldier's only response was to motion with his little finger for us to turn the car around and leave.

I stayed put. The soldier was annoyed and he startled us by pounding on the bonnet of our car with the full force of his hand. We could have yelled back, but we didn't. Confronted by a claim of fairness from an Israeli soldier, a member of an army that had been in occupation of our land for over thirty-seven years, who had destroyed our lives and brought us to the point of having to beg to be allowed to get back home in the evening after dinner, we were speechless.

Silently, I turned the car around and left.

We drove first down a new settler road towards the junction known as Eun el Haramieh (the Eyes of the Bandits), where travellers in Ottoman times used frequently to be waylaid and robbed. It was a long, straight road that bisected the countryside and rearranged it. The road signs indicated Israeli settlements: Shilo, Ofra, Dolev. There was hardly any mention of Arab towns, nor could any be seen. There was nothing to indicate to an Israeli driving along this road that there was an Arab presence on this land. It was as if these Israeli settlers had painted a reality for themselves, shielding all other realities from sight. It was what Israel had done to its Arab citizens, confining them to small ghettos and giving most of their land to their Jewish neighbours.

For safety, the whole road was lit up as though we were in a major city. It must have been phenomenally expensive to build these roads and keep them lit.

There were no other cars on the road. It was entirely desolate. That these roads had been built for people now too scared to use them was an oddly comforting thought. Most of the time, as I drove, I was not sure where I was. I couldn't see the landmarks I usually used to navigate my way back home. All I could see was the long road cutting through the darkness.

Then we saw a turn to the west, which we assumed was the road to Ramallah. We took it. Soon enough we came upon a mound of earth blocking our way. The road had been closed by the army. We could see the village of Silwad ahead of us. It was only a few kilometres north of Ramallah but we could not reach it. This road was not intended for the Palestinian residents of Silwad, nor were we expected to be on it. We backed up and continued along the main road. Finally we found what we assumed was the Atarah intersection. If this was it we would be just north of Birzeit, from where we could drive south to Ramallah. 'Halamish,' Penny said in triumph, reading the road sign, 'this is our crossroad.' Our new road markers were now Israeli settlements.

The road we took was no longer straight and it was unlit. The bushes at the sides were ominously high, thick and dark, and I was wondering more than ever whether we were wise to be driving at night along this road. What if a group of armed men should emerge from the bushes? There was nothing to distinguish our car at night from a settler's car. If we were shot it would be our fault for being so frivolous as to go to dinner in Jerusalem.

The fact that this road was unlit must have meant that it was not used by settlers. That was a comfort. But Penny remained silent. She told me later that it was there, on that stretch of road, that the friend of a driver we knew was killed.

As we drove uncertainly in the dark I wondered if we would come across an Israeli army jeep. We would be all alone with potentially murderous soldiers on this dark and empty road. My agitated mind revived the memory of the death of a relative soon after the occupation. He had been driving alone near the Latrun salient, close to the border with Israel. He was stopped by an army jeep and killed. The soldiers took his black-and-white-checked keffiyeh, dipped it in petrol from his car and set his corpse on fire. A few days later his burnt remains were found by a shepherd.

Fortunately we were spared any more meetings with the army. We drove slowly, unsure whether this road was ever going to get us home. I saw a yellow taxi approaching. I blinked my lights and called on him to stop before asking for directions. 'Continue straight until after the bridge and then take a dirt road to your right. That will get you to Birzeit,' the driver said, and sped away. We eventually found ourselves driving through the Arab town and, despite the lateness of the hour, the town's market was still open and young college couples from the university there were strolling in the tree-lined streets. We had come upon the people whose presence was shielded from the view of the colonisers, for whom they do not exist.

From Birzeit we drove without incident to Ramallah.

It was a terrifying drive. We were lucky that nothing happened. But I was glad to have had the experience. To have seen the countryside with its new security arrangements at night, to have heard this soldier speak about fairness, which only signalled how shut off from reality he was, to have seen writ on the land the fanaticism of its settlers, who deluded themselves by creating a land of make-believe where the history of one people had been utterly erased from the landscape and replaced by a messianic fantasy, all this was most edifying. It made me realise that Israel's settlement programme was a passing phenomenon and was not going to survive. Their presence was untenable, just as the Ottomans, after a 400-year presence here, also had to leave. But before they did, they destroyed our landscape, felling most of the trees to use for fuel during the First World War. How much damage would these settlers have done before they left?

Time is on the Palestinians' side, I thought, after I finished this harrowing drive. The Israelis had been inflexible, allowed to get away with their crimes because of the sympathy felt towards them because of the Holocaust. But this emotional dispensation would eventually run its course.

When I got home I remembered an entry I'd read in the diaries of Khalil Sakakini, who worked as an educational inspector under the British Mandate. In it he describes a trip he took on 13 December 1934: 'if the Jews have a few impoverished colonies the Arabs have thousands of villages. We travelled from Jerusalem to Hebron to Beir Sabaa to Gaza to Khan Yunus to Majdal to Ramle to Lydda to Kalkilia to Tul Karam and only passed through Arab lands. What is owned by the Jews compares as nothing to what is owned by the Arabs in Palestine.'

Meanwhile, to his surprise, the unseen people were organising, training and arming themselves, and when the time came they emerged from their 'invisible' locations, fought and won a war that ended up forcing out those who had only seen their own kind and failed to see the enemy in their midst. Sakakini too was forced out of his new home in Jerusalem, never to return.

Next morning as I was shaving, I looked at my face in the mirror. For the first time I felt ready to take responsibility for the way I looked. I realised that the contours of my face, the lines around my mouth, have mainly come from clenching my jaws from tension. This was no serene, relaxed face. There could no longer be any pretence or any concealment. I could see etched there the signs of my failures and successes.

The real suffering, the constant reminder and knowledge of the bloodshed inflicted on my people, weighed heavily on me and left its mark on my face. Mine was no longer a face with an elfish smile, as had been the case when my father was alive and I played the role of rebel son. Memory had wiped that smile from my face.

12

Shocking News

Ramallah, 2006

On the morning of 2 June 2006, I opened my email and found this message:

Raja,

I am sorry I have not been in touch since your uncle's wife died. Unfortunately, I have been having some medical problems.

About three months ago, I discovered my left eyelid was drooping, but the many tests I did did not uncover the cause. At the same time, I began losing weight, eating less and feeling without my usual bounce. In the last couple of weeks, my spleen became painfully swollen and my liver somewhat enlarged and I became breathless after any physical exertion. Suddenly my white blood cell count became very high, along with other blood work anomalies. I have just consulted a wonderful hematologist, Professor Debbie Rund (who was a social worker before becoming an MD), and together we

179

looked at my blood cells. She is fairly certain that I have a low-grade, non-Hodgkin's lymphoma. Thursday, I did a whole body CT, and on Sunday I will have a bone marrow and a pleural tap to remove fluid that has accumulated in my right lung and is the cause of the breathlessness. Along with other tests, specialized blood work, molecular genetics, immunoassay, etc., we should have a definitive diagnosis in the next week or two. I will then begin treatment. All my doctors were very optimistic about treatment and the prognosis; so that although my condition is serious, it appears highly treatable. There are 30 different subtypes of lymphoma, each with its own treatment (and a differential diagnosis with chronic lymphocytic leukemia, which is also treatable).

Great credit is to Iva, who felt that something was wrong, pushed me to continue checking things out and even suspected a hematological problem long before the doctors did. Her support has been, as you would imagine it to be, outstanding …

My spirits are good. I have been working as usual and even feeling more creative and more alive than usual …

I promise to keep you posted.

Henry

I immediately wrote back:

I had wished the silence was due to other psychological, political reasons, anything but that. Still, I am so glad to hear that your spirits are up. How strange that with the death of a parent (as was the case with your father) so many of my friends begin to have medical problems, as though the parent had held them in abeyance.

Keep me posted. I will be thinking of you. Tell me when you feel you would like to meet and I will come to Jerusalem at any time that is good for you. Your optimistic spirit will help you get over this. With your positive attitude and Iva's good care and love I have no doubt the treatment should work.

Much love and tender wishes,
Raja

Hearing about Henry's illness via email was nightmarish. As I read the details of what was happening to him I could hardly believe it. His body was falling apart. It was a horror story. For a perverse moment I dared to hope: could it all be an elaborate game to see how different people would react? After all, these were just written words, emails, a virtual reality. I had not seen anything with my own eyes. I longed to see him.

It wasn't a prank. It was even worse than I expected. Iva met me outside the door of their house and warned me not to be shocked.

Henry was on oxygen but he was cheerful. We did not speak about the disease. I had wanted to hear how he felt, what he was thinking. But he did not want to talk about it. I also wanted him to talk about what he wanted to talk about. As with politics, Henry was good at avoiding issues, but in this case I welcomed it. I did my best to tell him funny stories, to make him laugh, to entertain him and not to show how depressed

I actually felt. I'm glad that I went to see him, but sad that my first visit to his house should have been under these circumstances.

During the visit Henry introduced me to his eldest daughter. I remembered him telling me that Ella was the most Israeli of his children. She had accepted the draft without hesitation. She greeted me coldly. 'At last,' she said, and left the room.

When I arrived home, Ramallah was in mourning. The latest Israeli airstrike on the Gaza Strip had killed fourteen people in twenty-four hours, six from one family who last year had lost four of its members. Among the dead were two infants.

I wrote to Henry:

> From reading your last bulletin, I knew what you had been through before I came to see you. And to see your smiling face, to hear your happy melodious voice, was such a relief. I am so glad to have made the visit. When we shook hands, your grip was firm – I believe as firm as your spirits and will. And this is the most important of all. Please know you are constantly on my mind. Good vibrations can work miracles.

Henry responded:

> It did me well to see you – body and soul. Yes, when things are back to normal, we can do something all together with Penny. Even come up to your place or a tea party that I ridiculously suggested or …
>
> I have something else to tell you about the day

we met at the film festival in the Jerusalem Theatre.
Something else happened just before I met you. I will
tell you when we meet. I was speaking with Iva today
about what to do when I feel bad like I did Friday night
and I thought speaking with good friends. So with your
permission, I may turn to you at short notice to see if we
can meet and work the wonders of our friendship or just
have you read to me or watch *I Love Lucy* together or the
Mahabharata. Your vibrations are coming in loud and
clear and embrace me. I overcome my deepest fear of
abandonment.

I answered:

Any time, Henry. Nothing will please me more than to
know I can be of help in any small way to you during
your difficult time. You remain an inspiration in your
fortitude. I'm glad and relieved you're starting treatment.
I only hope it will not be too painful and depressing. But
you know to whom to turn when you need it.

A few days later, another message from Henry:

I remember well, that for years, my greatest joy
Was to bury the dead,
When I did field work (in every sense)
In a Jerusalem Burial Society (Chevra Kadisha)
In my time, I have buried many and
Myself many a time.
After each funeral,
I felt joyfully, painfully, alive,

Because I have lived
I will remember to die.
But not now Sweet Death, not now!

As I read this I thought of the grim but very real prospect of never again being able to go on walks with Henry. For many years the political situation made it difficult for us to walk together. It also made our communications limited and strained. Politics had narrowed me. It had reduced us. It had taken a terrible disease to remind me of how close I felt to Henry. It was our friendship that was important, not our political affiliations, not what we did, not what we failed to do.

Later I wrote to tell him that I was writing a book about walking in the Palestinian hills and this was bringing back the happy memories of the many walks we took together:

Do you remember when we stopped by one *qasr* [castle]? Do you remember that walk? You stood on the roof of that stone structure as the daylight turned to dusk. I stayed below looking up, saw you standing with your long beard, and I thought you looked like a prophet. The terraced hills were in the background. I waited to hear what you had to say. You remained standing with the light dimming behind you. As night began to fall, the silence was profound. Slowly you descended the circular inner stairs and emerged from the small door and came to join me. We both remained silent, taken by the beauty of the darkening hills all around us. Then you stooped down and began collecting old rusty utensils left over from the famers who had used that old structure.

And I thought, damn this political situation here that has prevented us from taking more of our most enjoyable walks. This is partly why I'm writing this book, to preserve the memory and hopefully make those who never took these walks experience something of the beauty and magic of this place.

May you get well soon,
Raja

That morning the body of a young man from the Jewish settlement of Itmar who was kidnapped and killed was found near to the spot which I had reminisced about to Henry in my note. Later, when the army came to recover the body, they were accompanied by a masked young man who had been arrested at a checkpoint near Ramallah. He had confessed everything to the police. At the time we were having a dinner party for Rema, a professor of anthropology at Birzeit University, who had just returned from Holland. We were enjoying the champagne she had brought. The army stormed into Ramallah and arrested Hamas legislators and ministers who had been renting flats not far from where we lived. Throughout we had no idea what was happening.

Even though the war against Gaza had begun, Penny and I still went to visit Henry at his house. Ilana, his sister, whom he loved dearly, was visiting. They were so close and such good friends. Henry and Iva had a tea party for us in their gorgeous garden – the tea party he had often spoken of, which we had never managed to have. Henry was dressed in a white suit, with white shoes and a white cowboy hat to protect himself from the sun. It made him look seraphic.

As he walked us out to our car he held my hand. How vulnerable he seemed. And yet the whole party was so well planned. He had spoken articulately and incessantly about the past, his parents, his relationship to his mother and his siblings. He was unstoppable. He spoke about very intimate things without reserve. At times he was abrupt with Iva, interrupting her when she tried to say something. But she didn't mind. She was being motherly, as she must have been towards him for many years. Sometimes Ilana interjected; she also disagreed with some of his conclusions. Henry was like me, allowing himself to get slightly carried away and make sweeping and emotional final conclusions. Ilana was more measured, rational.

He looked different now without his beard. He had lost weight. His eyes were a bit glossy. Occasionally he leaned back, trying to be sociable, letting others speak. But I got the impression that he didn't want us to make comparisons with our own experiences. This was his experience; he did not want interruption. So I listened without interrupting, reflecting on how long we had known each other and what we had been through together.

After the party I wrote:

Shocking News

Dear Henry,

It was a wonderful tea party, worth waiting for all these years. It felt very strongly out of time. Perhaps this is the only way to live in this place, times being so desolate.

It was as though we were continuing conversations started many years ago.

It was so good to see Ilana again and meet your daughters and of course see Iva, who was so kind and generous, as always.

Warm wishes, Raja

The medical bulletins Henry had been sending were long and elaborate and highly informative about the course of his treatment. But what surprised me was that in them he alluded to the security situation and compared his cancer treatment to a war. He had also been making more political references than he had ever done before. In one email he asked:

Why do we kill and kill and kill?
Is my physical state so interconnected to the battlefield?
This week I had no nausea from CHOP of MABTHERA (the
MABTHERA is a genetically modified monoclonal
antibody that specifically attacks B-cell with CD20+
antigen markers) but an Israeli
Targeted assassination missile murdered a woman and her
seven children:
How can that be called war

But bloody, bloody, bloody bloody, bloody, bloody, bloody
> *revenge*
Each side caring only for its domestic audience
And all their bloods crying out to us
From the Book of Genesis for generations,
Because killing once done, cannot be undone.
I discover scars on the top of my shaven head
As though in my shamanistic trip I, too, was
In a knife slashing, head bashing.
I recall as a child
A swing smashing into my made bloody head.
But after coming to a heart-stopping coma at five years old,
What power can a swing or shaman knife slashing have
> *over a ghost?*
I live in my new look.

His new beardless look was receiving a favourable response in some quarters. The best, he wrote, was from Jon Feder, the chief editor of an Israeli digital news page, who, as Henry reported, told him:

> I never knew you were such a handsome guy.
>
> Your face (your real face …) is of the manly but sensitive kind.
>
> You look determined–intent, but sensitive–exquisite, at the same time.
>
> Too bad you had to be beaten by cancer in order to let us all know what a good-looking guy you are.

Henry went on to write:

I think of my profound ambivalence to my appearance
especially since as a kid I relished and suffered from
being chronically called 'cute'. I yearned for an archetypal
masculine that led me to the path of the beard and the
Jewish wise old man tradition. What did I do to achieve
this ascribed look? If I were ugly, would I be loved less?
Yet I know so much of our attraction and sex life is based
on appearances which are both trivial persona and
profound Self all at once. Now, at last, I am a cute wise
one.

In the past I didn't see many Israeli Jewish men
with the yarmulke and tallit (fringed prayer shawl) in
the streets of Jerusalem; only the orthodox wore these
symbols of their religion. Now it was very common
to see the young wearing them as a public display of
association or affiliation unrelated to their moral or
ethical behaviour but simply to declare: I'm a Jew.

However, Henry's decision to wear a beard was
nothing like that.

Not long ago I was having lunch at the Ambassador
Hotel in East Jerusalem with an Israeli friend who
teaches law, whom I've known for a long time. He
reminded me of a walk we had taken with his wife and
three young children in the Ramallah hills. This was
in the early 1980s, when the settlement of Dolev had
just been established. I had said then something which
stuck in his mind to the effect that children would be
born to those settlers for whom these hills would be

home and how this was bound to complicate matters and lead to inevitable future tragedies.

Unlike Henry, this friend came from a strict orthodox family and in his attire and food habits followed orthodox traditions. For the longest time, ever since I've known him, he had a beard and wore a yarmulke. Then one day I saw that he had shaved his beard and stopped wearing a yarmulke. When I asked him whether he had stopped being religious, he replied, 'No, I'm still orthodox. It is not something one can give up. It's a way of life that I've been raised on.'

'Then why did you change?'

'Because I don't like to be associated any more with those who wear a yarmulke and a beard or with what they represent.'

Both these friends, for different reasons, have ended up losing their beards.

I was never one to go for national or religious symbols, never liked waving the flag or wearing the keffiyeh or a cross. Yet there was more to it than that. I was aware that one begins thinking it is possible to live many lives but ends up having to choose one and is distinguished and shaped by it.

Henry chose to live in Israel and this had enduring consequences. I choose to remain in Palestine and resist the injustice by fighting through the law and writing on certain subjects in a certain way. This has meant that other lives and other sorts of writings which I had hoped to do could not be done. A time will surely come when the memories of what I failed to do will come to haunt me.

Perhaps for Henry it was different. How he saw himself is best expressed by a poem he once sent me in which he wrote:

> I want to be untied
> Sailing like a kite set free
> Pushed by a wind, going no where

But can anyone live like that?

13

Israel at My Doorstep

Ramallah, 2009

As the years went by, the border closed in on us. Israel drew closer and closer to Ramallah. By January 2009, Israel was a mere five kilometres from my home. It had been ten years since I could walk in the valley near my house or drive down the road to A'yn Qenya, to enjoy the spring there.

It started in the summer of 1980. I stood with Jonathan Kuttab, the co-director of Al-Haq, on the summit of one of the hills above Ramallah, enjoying the view of numerous hamlets to the north. As we feasted our eyes on the hills rising and falling below us, like the ripples on a lake, we whispered to each other how beautiful it was lest we be overheard by covetous settlers who would grab this gorgeous hilltop for one of their settlements and deprive us of this view. Just a few months later our fears proved right. Work on the settlement of Dolev began and it became home to a few thousand Israelis. Yet even though we could not walk up the hill, we could still hike in the valleys below, undisturbed.

I remember discussing Dolev with Henry, who told me that it was a small settlement of peaceful, pious Jews, lovers of nature who had named their settlement after a biblical tree. They refused to surround it with barbed wire like other settlements. Why should they need to, they argued, when they wanted to live in peace with their neighbours? As settlements went I didn't think too badly of them, with their low, unobtrusive buildings that did not spoil the view.

Then came the first intifada.

The settlers from Dolev used to pass through Ramallah on their way to Beit Eil, the headquarters of the Israeli Civil Administration, where many of them worked. Their children went to school in a settlement also called Beit El. To avoid getting lost in Ramallah, the army had marked the settlers' path through our town with a yellow line. This was a clear violation of our space but I was willing to let it go. Then, when the intifada started, they had to employ an armed escort after people started to throw stones at them.

On 8 October 1990, after the massacre at Al Aqsa when Israeli police killed some twenty Palestinians and injured over 150, some settlers on their way home shot at the window where my wife was standing. Had Penny not ducked, the bullet would have struck her in the head. We kept the shrapnel as a memento mori.

On 26 March 1991 a Dolev settler, Yair Mendelssohn, was killed driving back to Dolev. It was claimed that a Palestinian had shot at his car, which had swerved down into a steep gully. For three days, 40,000 people were punished for the death of one

Dolev resident by being forced to stay at home, away from their work and schools. All along both sides of the road to their settlement, olive trees were felled for the security of the settlers, ancient stone walls were demolished and cars parked by the houses of Palestinian residents on Tireh Road were damaged by settler fire. We were then living on this road and were fearful of what the settlers might do next.

A little later, as I was walking in the area, I came across a bulldozer destroying centuries-old terracing and uprooting the olive trees there. I thought they might be widening the road, but shortly after, on another walk with two friends from the UK, we saw on the outskirts of Ramallah a large boulder painted with the words 'Yad Yair', which means 'Memorial for Yair'. It was high above the road, only eight kilometres north of Ramallah and on a plot of land that belonged to a resident of the city. It was a shrine dedicated to the memory of Yair Mendelssohn.

We noticed in the strata of the rocks at the side of the road, near where the boulder had been propped up, pockets of what looked like tubular rocks. I thought they must be fossilised roots. What else could have penetrated into the rock in this manner? I argued. I imagined that the roots had dug into the rock for support and in search of water, then remained embedded there for years, centuries, until they had become part of the rock. We scraped away a thin layer of soil and tried to pull out a piece. These round stumps, each as thick as a thumb, were not difficult to extract and I managed to get my piece, showed it to the others and kept it with me. We continued on our walk, but, as we turned the corner, an army jeep stopped abruptly and the soldiers came down carrying their weapons.

'What are you doing here?' one of them asked us.

He had thick curly black hair and wore a purple T-shirt underneath his army fatigues. His socks were also purple. He had a soft, almost shy look in his eyes, very unlike the glazed stare of the professional soldier. Clearly he was only a reservist.

He could not understand what we were doing in the hills. He looked at us and said, 'This is a closed area.' Then, pointing to me, 'He knows this.'

I refrained from saying anything. The soldier did not seem to take much interest in me. He was trying to figure out the other two, the English man and woman who were so bold as to be walking unarmed in these hills, where they could easily be mistaken for settlers and harmed.

'This is a closed military area. You cannot come here without permission,' he said.

As he spoke, I felt my thumb-like fossil and remembered that it amounted to a weapon. The soldier was bound to keep it as evidence of my hostile intent should I be arrested. Under Israeli military law, stone-throwing was a serious offence.

Shortly after that incident, the army set up an outpost and road barrier there, stopping cars and pedestrians using the road. Then the army expropri-ated hundreds of acres of privately owned land south of the outpost, reaching to the last houses on the out-skirts of Ramallah. The land had been surrounded by barbed wire with no compensation paid to the owners. Our hills were being prepared for yet another Jewish settlement. I had witnessed this process before in other parts of the West Bank. This time it was only a short distance from where I lived.

I also discovered that the fossil I had extracted from the area was not the petrified root of a tree but coral. There had been a reef once close to where I lived. Water had submerged this area long before Arabs or Jews settled here.

After the Oslo Accords, the settlers from Dolev stopped using the road with the yellow line. Instead they raised funds from their supporters in the United States to construct a road that cut through the valley and the hills connecting their settlement north-west of Ramallah with Beit El to the east. That winding road, which was illegal, scarred the land, destroying much of the beauty in the wadi and along the terraced hills. The Israeli army deemed the road too dangerous and prohibited the settlers from using it, replacing it with a wider and better-designed road to the north that caused even more damage to the Ramallah hills.

This was a time of extensive Israeli settlement. The number of Jewish settlers in the West Bank more than doubled. Most of this took place in what the Oslo Accords designated as Area C, comprising more than half of the West Bank. The area around Yad Yair did not fall within that category, but when the Israeli government began at the start of the new century to construct a wall around the West Bank the settlers in Dolev became concerned that they might be stranded on the Palestinian side of the barrier. They increased their efforts to raise more money to build a network of illegal settlements that now dot the hills north of Ramallah and form a ring around the city.

Years earlier I had asked a resident in the village of A'yn Qenya in the valley adjacent to Dolev whether they were being harassed by the settlers.

'No,' he said. 'They live their lives and we live ours.'

'Do they pass through the village?' I asked.

'Yes. Every morning, very early. Before sunrise they drive through towards Ramallah. They seem to have a place of worship up on the hills near Ramallah. They drive up and stay there until sunrise, then drive back.'

I wondered about this. I had been feeling that our hills were spared more settlements because there was no mention of Ramallah in the Bible and so any claim to possess this land on religious grounds would be a stretch. What I hadn't realised was that the Yad Yair shrine was turning into a new place of worship – much as the grave of Baruch Goldstein, who murdered twenty-nine Palestinian worshipers at the Ibrahimi Mosque in Hebron in 1994, had become a venerated site.

I was able to find out how the settlers felt about their place and mine on these hills when in May 2008 I took a walk with Quil Lawrence from the BBC. We started from Mizraa Qiblia and went down to A'yn Qenya. Just as we reached the centre of the village a car stopped. A man with a yarmulke was at the wheel and next to him another with side locks. Quil greeted them in Arabic. The driver rolled down his window and asked what we were doing here. I thought he had mistaken us for Israelis who had lost our way.

'We live near here,' I said.

'Where?'

'In Ramallah.'

'What are you doing here?'

'We live near here.'

He could see Quil recording the conversation.

'You are recording me?' he asked.

Quil said he was a journalist.

'Do you have a card?' he asked. Then, 'Let's call the army. I don't need your card.'

We were being interrogated by someone with no authority to do any such thing, so I asked, 'Who are *you*?'

'I am no one.'

'Why are *you* here?'

In his poor English he answered, 'I'm different from you. I'm living here. Really living here, not just like you.'

'What does "not just like you" mean?'

The settler, who lived in Dolev on the hill just above where we stood, didn't answer and proceeded to call the army on his mobile phone. He had their number. They were his army and were there to protect him against me. They would respond to his call, not to mine. The area was off bounds to the Palestinian police and technically, by walking in these hills without a permit from the Israeli military authorities, I was breaking the law.

A Palestinian van driver stood nearby. He had been wondering throughout this exchange whether we were settlers, but then he recognised me because he had once given me a lift.

'Just come into the van and leave him alone,' he said, indicating the Jewish driver. 'I know him well and he is always making trouble.'

We got in. The settler drove ahead and tried to block the road with his car. After some five minutes, he thought better of it and moved away. Further up the alternative dirt road that had been opened by the villagers on their own initiative after the closure of the older road leading from Ramallah to the village we found three jeeps that had created a mobile checkpoint, but it was only stopping people entering A'yn Qenya and we passed through unchecked.

The van driver said he might get into trouble. The man we had encountered was a notorious settler called Flicks, who always came to the village, blocked the road, threw stones at the houses and once threw fruit juice at young men standing by the side of the road. He always went through town on his way to pray at Yad Yair.

The words of the settler stayed with me: 'I'm different from you. I'm living here. Really living here.' He had that glint in his eye as if he knew something that I didn't. What could it be? Did he think he had a special dispensation from God?

A few months later I saw cars passing along the

old road to A'yn Qenya that had been closed for many years. It looked as though the road had been completely reopened. I walked to Yad Yair to see what had become of it. It was deserted. Metres of barbed wire, cleared and levelled land, cement blocks. That was all. I saw a sign with 'Yad Yair' on it in Hebrew. I thought I should get my camera and photograph it. Then I saw another wooden sign that had been thrown on the ground. On it in Hebrew were the words, 'Blessed are those who come to Yad Yair.' I thought I would take this back with me as a souvenir, but when I bent down to pick it up my heart began to pound and I began hyperventilating. By stepping down to pick up this placard belonging to the illegal settlement I was attempting to break a huge barrier of fear that had been gathering over many years. I was all alone on the site, there was no reason to feel afraid and yet I couldn't help myself. My body was shaking like a leaf. I lifted up my head and stood there under the clear blue sky trying to breathe deeply. When I finally regained control over myself, a profound sense of defeat came over me. I realised I could no longer walk on this land without feeling that I was crossing into forbidden territory.

A short time passed and it was as though Yad Yair had never been. The outpost had been the initiative of a few families from Dolev and was not incorporated in the larger plan for Jewish settlements in the area. Because it was situated on a steep hill so close to Ramallah, the army was not interested in preserving it. They moved their base closer to Dolev and decided to dismantle the outpost. The settlers claimed that in doing so the army had 'desecrated' the land. 'We are certain that we will return and settle Yad Yair through our determination and patience,' they vowed. 'The army will not frighten us, nor prevent us from reaching [Yad Yair].' Grass and weeds were all there was now. Nature was already beginning to take over, as nature always does.

The Jewish settlers didn't give up. On 29 July 2012, the eve of Tisha B'Av 5772 , a day of fasting commemorating the destruction of the Temple in Jerusalem, a number of them came to the site and proceeded to 'recite mournful odes for the destruction of the Temple' from the Book of Lamentations. The *Jewish Press*, an American weekly newspaper based in Brooklyn, New York, claimed that around fifty men, women and children had attended. Another photograph attached to the report showed two men with a small number of children. The young man in the foreground was wearing sandals and shorts. His wheat-coloured face had a tight-lipped, sombre expression. He closely resembled the son of a builder who did some work for me at the house, who looked just as unhappy. Much as I tried to find out why the builder's son was taciturn, I couldn't get him to speak. Perhaps this young man in the picture was hoping to find satisfaction and fulfilment from becoming observant. His head was bent over the Torah, which he clutched in his hands intently.

The slightly older man, bespectacled and also wearing an air of sadness, seemed like a caring father embracing two younger children. He read to them from a book. He did not look sinister, but paternal and mentoring. It was an intimate portrait of a loving father showing his kids the way and of an older boy, perhaps a disaffected neighbour or a brother, who had also come along. Except for where they sat, I would have admired the intimacy of this scene.

In another report, while decrying the role of the army in destroying this outpost, the settlers emphasised its strategic importance in blocking the spread of Ramallah, my city.

14

Lunch at Everest

Beit Jalla, 2013

We felt a great sense of achievement and relief when we reached the Everest Restaurant. To get there we each had to take a different route, depending on whether we were Israeli or Palestinian. Even though it was July 2013 and many years had passed since the second intifada, Israel had not revoked the restrictions on our movements. The Palestinians had to wait for forty minutes at the Qalandia checkpoint. Our Israeli friends, on the other hand, had to take the road from Jerusalem to Gush Etzion, passing through a short tunnel and then over the longest bridge in Israel. They had to drive next through another, much longer tunnel under the Palestinian city of Beit Jalla and through a checkpoint that allows only Israeli traffic to pass. They continued straight until they reached a roundabout where they doubled back before reaching another checkpoint, turned right and followed the road to the settlement of Har Gilo. But before reaching the settlement, they had to take another right turn into Beit

Jalla. They then drove all the way up to the Everest Restaurant, located on the highest point in the area.

We were about twenty-five people and we were there to celebrate the release of Judy's grandson Natan from five and a half months in prison for refusing to serve in the Israeli army. But there was another reason for the gathering, which we had to keep secret from Judy. It was her eighty-fifth birthday. The reason we had chosen this venue was because it was the only place in the West Bank where Palestinians and Israelis could meet without the Israelis going through a checkpoint with a red sign forbidding them from entering a Palestinian city.

Natan was a slight, unassuming young man whose great influence, he said, was his grandfather Haim, who had left his studies at Harvard to volunteer for the Palmach. He had been drafted into the US army, serving from 1944 to 1946, and his encounter with the extermination camps in Europe led him to support the Zionist cause. But he was wounded during fighting in Palestine and returned to Harvard a blind man. Still, he managed to complete his doctorate in linguistics and published a study of the languages used by Muslims, Jews and Christians in Baghdad.

We were all curious to hear from Natan what he thought about the Israeli army and why he had decided to refuse the draft. For someone so young, he was highly articulate, telling us that he was not a pacifist but a conscientious objector. I had read an interview with him in *Haaretz* in which he told the reporter:

It is essential to be obstinate and speak your truth, down to the last comma. That is the only thing that can influence society when it must decide on issues of principle and forgo manipulation. I am against lying. Lying is wrong in every situation – and especially in the case of military service. The IDF really likes to get people who refuse to serve to say, 'I am depressed-crazy-handicapped, etc.' So it is important to underscore that my refusal does not stem from mental reasons.

He made it clear that his refusal was not intended to prompt more soldiers to dodge the draft. After all, he came from a family whose members had all served in the Israeli army. When he was asked whether he was disappointed that few Israelis were following his example, he replied:

Throughout, my actions have been dictated solely by my conscience. My refusal is not intended to get more soldiers to do the same but to emphasise that, as an Israeli citizen, I acted according to my conscience. The fact that I am alone just now in thinking this way and acting on it is also fine. I am disappointed to some extent in Israeli society – the fact that much of it does not agree about the actions that need to be taken to stop the occupation and our rule over another nation.

We showered him with questions about his experiences in prison, where he had worked in the kitchen.
'The hardest part was not knowing when it would be
over,' he said. When we asked how the other prisoners
reacted to him, he told us, 'I was able to make friends
with some of them. They were curious to hear from
me because they had never encountered someone with
ideas and positions like mine. But by the end I was glad
it was over.'

As Natan spoke, his grandmother looked at him,
her face full of pride – not because he shared her
politics but because he clearly showed that he had a
mind of his own. He had also probably inherited from
her his stubbornness and singularity. At no point did
Judy stop visiting her Palestinian friends in the West
Bank. Neither the intifada nor any red sign posted
at the checkpoint forbidding Israelis from going into
Palestinian areas ever deterred her. She was ready, as
few Israelis were, to break the law because she didn't
believe in it. She also helped wherever she could by
using her car to transport Palestinian children who
needed dialysis at Israeli hospitals and who could not
cross the checkpoint because their mothers would
not be allowed through. She was always there for her
friends, and it made no difference whether they were
Palestinian or Israeli.

I first met Judy in 1982 after the publication of my
book *The Third Way* and we have been friends ever
since. At her dinner parties she introduced me to other
like-minded friends, among them Reuven Kaminer,
whose granddaughter Tair was another conscientious

objector. Tair spent more than 100 days in military prison in 2016.

Judy had a dancer's poise and a great deal of charm. She graciously attended to everyone, and always managed to find out what other people were interested in, asking them questions and deflecting the conversation away from herself.

We always discussed politics, not only what was taking place but what action was needed. Sometimes we fought bitterly. After the Oslo Accords, some of her friends – former members of the Communist Party – argued passionately in favour of the deal. I disagreed. On other occasions I would find myself furiously venting my anger at the Israelis for what their military were doing. I knew I was being unfair and that Judy certainly was against the army's actions, yet she never became visibly angry. She listened patiently – she was always a good listener – and sometimes she made comments which only later, when I had cooled down, did I understand. But she never stopped me or took offence.

At lunch I found myself wondering for the first time to what extent immigrants from North America like Judy become Israeli after moving there. Judy was from an assimilated New York family that was not Zionist. She once told me that coming to Israel was for her like a shot in the dark. 'I was twenty-five. I met Haim Blanc at Harvard and he asked me if I would go to Palestine with him. I refused. So he went alone and then he came back and asked me again. This time I decided to risk it and join him. I arrived in Israel six years after the state was established.'

At the beginning she felt at sea. 'But I survived,' she said, which I interpreted to mean she had stuck to her own beliefs and ways. She did it by raising a family and cultivating Israeli and Palestinian friends. She did not mingle with Palestinians for selfish reasons, to clear her conscience. She was like Henry in that regard, but unlike him she was always eager to be politically involved. She wanted to change the status quo. It was in the Blanc home that the Committee for Solidarity with Birzeit University and the Committee Against the War in Lebanon were formed. Sharp and full of vitality, Judy was one of the women who in December 1988 started Women in Black, holding vigils every Friday at which they carried 'Stop the Occupation' posters in Hagar Square in Jerusalem and endured the hostility of passers-by.

She had met Henry and knew about our friendship. She sometimes invited us together to her house, but the two of them were not close. Both possessed strong personalities and were independent. Judy never stopped being an American in Israel and Henry never stopped being Canadian. But their children will be Israeli, even if they do become dissidents.

At the Everest Restaurant gathering, we soon left Natan alone. Khalil Mahshi, who worked for UNESCO in Paris, was there with his wife, Suhair Azouni. He described how as a child he would come here with his uncle, who played the oud. It used to be a happy, peaceful place. So many wonderful parties had been held here under the pine trees.

Even at these tense times, the place was tranquillity

itself, with a slight breeze passing through the pine needles – a natural canopy over the long table that Rita Giacaman, an old, close friend of Judy's and ours, had insisted on having the waiters place outside on the porch. A dog – it was Judy's son Jeremiah's – sniffed around happily as the group took their seats around the long lunch table. We drank to Judy's health. Penny stood up and read an ode she had composed for Judy:

A poet I am not, more's the pity,
My ode to Judy is more like a ditty,
But from a friend's heart if not a bard's brain,
Even if for each rhyme I must strain.
I celebrate here a friendship in verse –
Judy, Penny and Rita in good times and worse.
During Gulf War I, Judy would telephone:
Dears, sirens sounding, there may be trouble.
Sirenless, Ramallah was then not a bubble!
Early second intifada, Judy listened to Mozart.
Irritated at his cheerfulness, she had to part
For a while, but who can resist him for long?
Even Rita, a Bach fan, got swept by his song.
Remembering the past with Judy is a pleasure,
But our present moment here is something to
*   treasure.*
And for more words, I turn to the rest
Of you here, with one last word on the past
Before Judy takes a bow
Sung by old B. Dylan, his guitar ablast:
We were so much older then,
We're younger than that now.

Khalil spoke about the special relationship he'd always had with Judy and how close to her he felt. He mentioned how, during his time as a professor at Birzeit University when the military would not allow mail to reach him, Judy let him use her West Jerusalem mailbox to receive books he had ordered from abroad. He also spoke of their struggle to have the university opened after it had been closed by the military during the first intifada.

I spoke of touring Europe with Judy and Reuven Kaminer in the early 1980s to speak about the danger of continued settlement building. I told our audiences how Reuven kept saying that the Jews were escaping from a house on fire by throwing themselves out of the windows and falling on the shoulders of the Palestinians. Standing next to Reuven, I was the Palestinian who had to describe to our European audiences what the consequences of this were, on me and on my people. This experience strengthened our relationship and helped it to endure.

In retrospect, even the most traumatic times yield good stories. Some even brought tears of laughter to our eyes. We remembered the thrill of more hopeful times when we were certain we would succeed and the long years of despair that followed. We laughed at how Rita could not survive without the Israeli soured cream *shamenet* and how Judy had to slip through checkpoints to keep her well stocked. Some of those friends who used to gather at Judy's West Jerusalem flat to discuss politics are sadly no longer with us, but those of us who remained had a wealth of memories.

On this joyful occasion we tried to concentrate on the happy ones. Then, striking a more serious note, Rita said, 'People sometimes praise Judy and me for coming together from our two different sides – but we are on the same side.'

Now it was the turn of Sarah, Judy's only daughter, to speak. As she drew to the end, she paused and then added in a thoughtful tone of voice, 'I was not aware that I have two sisters, Penny and Rita.' After she said this I looked around at Judy's children, especially at Sarah, who seemed the worrying type. I thought about how much I enjoyed Judy as a friend but how different it must be for her children, especially for Sarah as a daughter. It can't be easy to have a mother who takes such risks, who is always breaking the law and going to where many think it is too dangerous to go, especially for a woman at her advanced age.

Henry was not with us that day, but he and I had been meeting since. He had suffered terribly from the lymphoma, but he survived. During our meeting on 10 November 2015 he told me that, despite the fear of a recurrence, he felt more alive than ever. We spent several hours talking, exchanging news and catching up. As we talked, we walked in the green valley that overlooked the Arab neighbourhood of Silwan, where the most extreme Israeli Jews had tried to take over Palestinian homes one at a time to rebuild the ancient City of David. As I looked over the valley, I wondered whether it would have been possible for the

Israeli people to create a presence and a history for themselves here without negating ours. All evidence indicated they couldn't. But until they accept that the land must be shared and that both peoples have the right to self-determination, peace will remain elusive.

Naomi and I continued to meet whenever she came to Israel to see her mother and brother in the Galilee. And I would see her when I travelled to the UK. In 2015 I was attending a literary festival in London and Naomi came from her university in Warwick to hear me speak. It was lovely to see her. Afterwards we continued chatting to the very last minute before we had to go our separate ways. When she got back she wrote:

> Someone once said to me that when one meets old, real friends one is reminded of, and feels in touch with, who one really is. That is how it felt for me, not just from our all too brief chat, but from what you said, and how, on stage. Ran to catch my train (which I did, just) feeling hugely uplifted.

At our last meeting Henry gave me his book on siblings, *Brothers and Sisters*. In it he uses his vast knowledge of the Bible to write about these relationships. These days, what with messianic Zionism being used to justify all sorts of land theft, racism and even murder, and with Islam used to justify the most gruesome killings, I was curious to know where Henry stood on religion. His answer comforted me: 'I'm not a believer but I have a deep interest in tradition.

That's why, for example, I light a Shabbat candle. This is usually done by the woman in the house, but Iva comes from such an anti-religious home that she refuses to do it, so I do it and I offer a prayer for peace – not to God, because I don't believe, but just generally for peace in Jerusalem.'

I relished the time I spent with Henry. I would hate to lose him. Over the years our friendship had gone through many trials but the important thing was that it had endured.

After the joy of Judy's birthday celebrations, a series of atrocities and wars have followed each other in unholy succession. We then found ourselves once again embroiled in a third uprising, this time called a *habeh*, which began in October 2015.

Penny had just returned from a brief visit to Cairo. Together we hired a taxi to drive us to Jerusalem, where we were launching an anthology that we had both edited called *Shifting Sands: The Unravelling of the Old Order in the Middle East*. It was supported by the Edinburgh Book Festival and had come out of five panels presented there a year earlier. Nick Barley, the festival's director, had travelled here for the occasion, but we were unsure whether we would be able to make it to Jerusalem and whether we would have an audience. The Israeli army had placed concrete blocks at the entrance to many of the streets leading to the Palestinian quarters. I would have liked to invite Henry to the launch, but it was taking place at the Kenyon Institute in Sheikh Jarrah in East Jerusalem and it would not have been safe for him to come.

The taxi driver had turned on the local Palestinian radio station, which broadcast poems and songs urging protest and encouraging resistance. The mood was reminiscent of the first intifada, in which both Penny and I had enthusiastically participated. It reminded me how eloquent and creative our people became whenever their spirit of resistance was revived. But this uprising was different. There was no unified leadership guiding these young men and women, most of them born after the Oslo Accords. The mainly young Palestinians were staging demonstrations at checkpoints, but they had no political platform or concrete demands. They simply improvised ways of resisting. Some of these were non-violent, others violent, involving the stabbing of not only soldiers but also innocent Israelis. They protested and they threw stones at the soldiers. The Israeli government responded with violence, defining all resistance as terrorism. They shot back at the stone throwers, wounding and killing a number of them. Many were detained, including children in their early teens. The military took yet more measures to make our lives in the Occupied Territories more restrictive, increasing the number of road obstacles and making the crossing to and from Israel ever more difficult. This time the world, which once showed an interest, was distracted by its own problems, with the terror and criminality of the so-called Islamic State. If, in the first intifada, the media had helped place some restraints on the Israeli army, this was not the case now.

Cabinet ministers and law enforcement officials in Israel openly encouraged ordinary citizens to carry weapons and use them to kill attackers or those suspected of attacking Israelis rather than make arrests. The Palestinians who were shot were often left to bleed to death.

By Easter week 2016, six months after the *habeh* began, thirty Israelis had lost their lives and over 200 Palestinians had lost theirs. Thousands were imprisoned, including over 400 children. Abdel Fattah al-Sharif, twenty-one, from the occupied old city of Hebron, lay on the ground shot after he allegedly tried to stab an Israeli soldier. Sergeant Elor Azaria, eighteen, from the mixed Palestinian-Israeli city of Ramle, arrived at the scene. A member of the Israeli army's medical corps, instead of administering first aid to the bleeding Palestinian, he cocked his rifle and shot him point blank in the head.

I looked at a photograph of al-Sharif's body covered with a black cloth, the blood pooling under him, while soldiers and settlers milled around unconcerned. I could not bring myself to watch the video taken by a brave Palestinian of what had happened. Yet ever since this killing I could not stop thinking about the twisted ideology that had turned a young man into someone capable of killing a wounded man only a few years older than himself. His words: 'This terrorist must die.' What brutality and fear had blunted his humanity to such a degree that he had shown no compassion or hesitation. After the killing, he was so unrattled that he had the wherewithal to send a text message to his father informing him of his action.

I kept looking at this young man's face, searching

for clues. His large black eyes had an inquisitive look, but there was a superiority, an arrogance, an imperviousness to his expression. From the way his family hugged him, there was no indication that they had any doubt about the morality of their son's action, sparing no thought for the parents of the murdered young man, his family or friends. Nor did the majority of the Israeli public, who considered him a hero. Thousands went on to the streets to demonstrate on his behalf. Sixty per cent of young people expressed their belief that he had done the right thing by killing the Palestinian. The prime minister, Benjamin Netanyahu, called his family to express his support. Who, then, would help this young soldier to regain his humanity? What would it take to rehumanise the tens of thousands of desensitised Israelis like him?

To this turmoil, the fear-mongering Netanyahu had only one solution. He said, 'At the end, in the State of Israel, as I see it, there will be a fence that spans it all. I'll be told, "This is what you want, to protect the villa?" The answer is yes. Will we surround all of the State of Israel with fences and barriers? The answer is yes. In the area that we live in, we must defend ourselves against the wild beasts.'

By 'the State of Israel' Netanyahu meant all of Greater Israel, including the occupied West Bank.

As the *habeh* continued, it became more and more difficult to make the crossing between Israel and the West Bank.

When Penny and I had a late-night event in Jerusalem on a balmy evening in 2015 we decided to sleep over. We made sure to get to Jerusalem by twilight. I enjoy watching the night sky after the sun sets and before it gets dark, when the sky turns the most exquisite colour, a deep blue-green that we don't see in Ramallah. I have often argued with Penny over this. My belief is that the combination of the desert air from the east and the slightly humid air from the west produces this special effect in Jerusalem.

I woke up early the next morning and stood on the balcony of our room at the Ambassador Hotel overlooking the walled Old City. For a number of years after the occupation, the Israeli army had commandeered this hotel building and turned it into their headquarters. The view was superb. It looked deceptively peaceful, the light reflecting off the limestone buildings, the greenery between the low houses. It had a pastoral air to it that seemed at odds with the tension and hardship the people here had to endure.

I remembered what an Israeli acquaintance of my father from the time of the British Mandate once told him. It was just a few days after the end of the 1967 war and he was standing perhaps at the exact spot where I stood now and saw an Arab man coming down the street carrying a white umbrella. This Israeli could hardly believe his eyes. He must have been excited, tired and anxious so soon after the war and there in front of him was a member of the vanquished nation ambling along, carrying an umbrella because he was concerned about the effect of the sun on his skin. The Israeli chuckled at the incongruous sight.

Perhaps the thought crossed his mind that these people would not be too difficult to control. Why not take over the whole city and make it ours for ever? It couldn't possibly be hard to keep such people under our rule.

Having the Palestinian Territories under Israeli control made them imperious. I was reminded of Ya'akov Yehoshua, who became a government official after the occupation of East Jerusalem in June 1967. When Ishaq Musa al-Hussayni, a childhood friend from school and university, wrote asking for his help, Yehoshua wrote back, 'It seems that you have not yet grasped the new concept of the Jew – the creature that you disdained in the past has become a brave warrior, a tank soldier, a pilot …'*

So much happened so quickly and the Israelis saw what they could get away with. Less than a month after the war, when they annexed East Jerusalem, the world was tolerant of this breach of international law. They began to grab our land and to build settlements in East Jerusalem, the West Bank and the Gaza Strip and the world remained tolerant. And so began the de facto annexation of most of the occupied West Bank. They could reinterpret international legal conventions as they pleased, they could label all criticism as anti-Semitic, they could bomb Palestinians from the air,

---

*Quoted in Menachem Klein, *Lives in Common: Arabs and Jews in Jerusalem, Jaffa and Hebron* (Hurst & Co., London, 2014), p. 189.

they could take their land and water, and they could get away with it. Because the world would be tolerant.

Over thirty years ago, Henry and I sat at the crest of a hill overlooking Ramallah, talking about our friendship for an ITV television programme on friendships across political divides. We agreed to do the interview because we wanted to let the world know what was possible between the sons of our two nations and to warn against the settlement project that would destroy, if it were allowed to continue, all prospects of peace. A few years later, on that very spot where we had sat, settlers from nearby Dolev tried to establish Yad Yair. It was as though the hills we both loved and that had brought us together were becoming the curse that would separate us.

Henry and I do not look alike. But many Arabs and Jews, especially Sephardic Jews, are very similar in looks to Palestinians and so the two can be confused. Indeed, in the early weeks of the current 'outburst', a number of Yemini Jews took to wearing T-shirts which read: 'I'm a Yemini Jew', to avoid being mistaken for Arabs and attacked. And at the Hebrew University in Jerusalem Arab workers were made to wear coloured tags to identify them. When Nadera Shalhoub-Kevorkian, a professor of criminology at the university, asked one of her colleagues whether he appreciated what this meant, making the Arabs wear yellow tags, he corrected her saying, 'But they're not yellow, they're orange.'

On a recent trip to Berlin I visited the Jewish Museum. Looking at the relics of Jewish families who had once lived in Berlin, the fine porcelain plates and silver cutlery and tableware, I felt I couldn't go on with the visit. This was not only because of the sadness they inspired but also because the thought struck me that similar mementoes from Palestinians who had once lived in Jaffa and other Palestinian cities could fill many a similar museum. I stood there before these exhibits struggling to reject the comparison. The owners of these objects were killed in the most gruesome manner. The Nakba could not be equated with the Holocaust. For a start, many of the Jews who lived in Germany were annihilated, whereas most of the Palestinians went into exile. It is never right to conflate tragedies, but it is also wrong to use one tragedy to justify another, as Israeli propagandists have done.

A friend of mine was having dinner at the house of his Israeli friends in the German Colony in West Jerusalem. He told his friends that he had just been to Germany and was impressed by the Stumble Stones that had been installed in 500 towns and cities across the country. These were brass plates identifying where Jews once lived and worked. His friends agreed that this was an excellent way to commemorate what had befallen the Jews in Germany. But then when he suggested that similar markers might be placed by houses where Palestinians once lived there was complete silence.

The failure to acknowledge past atrocities is key to what is happening today, key to the crimes committed by the Jewish settlers. So worried is Israel by the memory of the Nakba that in March 2011 the Israeli Knesset passed the Nakba Law, depriving any state-funded body that commemorated the Nakba of its budget. In this way, Israel is attempting to erase the memory of the most traumatic event in Palestinian history.

Memory is political in Israel and Palestine. What to remember? Who to remember? These questions should be asked by both sides, Israeli and Palestinian. The answers will determine our common future in this land and whether or not we will ever have peace.

The Palestinians have to accept that after the Holocaust many countries refused to take in European Jews. For many, Palestine was their last refuge. Israelis have to remember the Nakba, withdraw from the Occupied Territories and acknowledge the brutality they have used against Palestinians struggling for self-determination and basic human rights.

Yet even when we Palestinians have our sovereign state, and one day we will, and Israel recognises our right of return, lasting peace requires that the victims of the conflict rise above their hatred and their pain, and that they forgive. It will require forgiveness from those who were hit the hardest by the occupation and by the Nakba, from those who have spent decades of their lives in refugee camps, from those who lost relatives, who were orphaned, who were maimed, who were made into collaborators, who saw their children burned alive by Israeli extremists. And it will require forgiveness from Israeli Jews who had relatives or children killed in senseless acts of violence in cafés and schools.

A lot has changed since my first meeting with Henry in Tel Aviv in 1977. I remember thinking then how Israel had character. I believed that Israel adhered to the rule of law and this was what made it strong. I then dedicated myself to promoting the rule of law in my own society and trying to hold Israel accountable for any violations of international law. All the work I did was based on my belief that international law would ultimately prevail.

It was during this latest *habeh* that I came upon a photograph in the local press of Israel's deputy foreign minister, Tzipi Hotovely, taking a tour of the controversial area east of Jerusalem known as E1. Israel was under pressure from the international community not to resume building settlements there and complete the encirclement of East Jerusalem and its total separation from the rest of the West Bank. She was present to support the resumption of building by settlers, which was illegal under international law, and to make sure that no Palestinian construction, which she called illegal, would be allowed to take place there. That very same day there was news of large numbers of illegal buildings newly constructed in Jewish settlements. There seemed to be a glint of triumph in Hotovely's gaze.

Meanwhile, the Sephardi Chief Rabbi declared that non-Jews should not be allowed to live in the land of Israel. It reminded me of Dov Baker, a yeshiva student from the illegal settlement of Gush Etzion near

Hebron, who told the *Guardian* in November 2015, 'This is our land. We need to be able to feel safe.' I had heard something similar from the Dolev settler who also challenged my right to the land, saying, 'I'm living here. Really living here.' I will not dispute these two men's attachment to the land, but that it should lead to exclusive possession and my eventual expulsion I cannot possibly accept. If the possession of land were based on religious feelings, the world would be in perpetual strife.

I think back on my various crossings over the past four decades to meet Henry, whether in 1977 or during the first and second intifadas. Whenever Henry and I were together we bonded and enjoyed each other's company, whether we were taking a walk or sipping a drink at the American Colony Hotel. It was as if in meeting we transcended our identities: he one of the oppressors and I one of the oppressed. When I went to Jerusalem to see him we met in a world of our own. We were simply two friends.

At the same time, each crossing would remind me of what I tried to forget when we met and this often made me feel resentful and angry towards Henry and his obliviousness of what it took for me to meet him. But maybe he was not as oblivious as I thought. Perhaps he agonised more than I realised.

In our small way, our friendship exposed the lie peddled by Netanyahu and his followers to Israeli people and to the world – that the Arab is the fundamental and eternal enemy of the Jew, that the conflict between Palestinian Arabs and Israeli Jews cannot be resolved diplomatically and that the Israeli people have to live forever by the sword.

It would be a fine thing if our friendship became the norm rather than the exception. One day this could happen, but until then I will not make its existence contingent on the elusive peace between Israelis and Palestinians.

Our lives are so intertwined with politics that I have all too often allowed myself to be defined by national affiliations. Seeing my friendship with Henry solely through the prism of the nation to which he belongs, I almost lost him for ever. I belong to my nation and have tried to play a role in moving its cause forward. Henry has never consented to the Israeli occupation and to Israel's brutal behaviour towards the Palestinians. He tried to see the best in everyone. He saw Palestinians as fellow human beings, as brothers and sisters. He also saw Jews as believers in tradition, as humane. Yet he is not a leader in his community, nor am I in mine.

Henry and I will continue to disagree. I know there will be more times when I feel disappointed with him and he with me, and perhaps there will be some anger.

I was tempted to ask him when we last met, 'Now that you have seen what Israel has become, do you ever regret coming to live here?' But this would have been the wrong question to ask. Despite the violence, the danger, the rise of extreme right-wing political parties and the racism, how could someone who has built his entire life here feel that it was all a mistake? How could he wish that he had never come here, that he had never met his wife, whom he loves dearly and only met because he came here?

We cannot unpick our life or the history of our nation. If I care for my friend I have to accept his decision and what he has made of his life. Had he not come here we would not have met and I would never have had a friend who has enriched my life as Henry has done. Despite what separates us, I am proud to have a friend called Henry.

Acknowledgements

Think where man's glory most begins and ends,
And say my glory was I had such friends.

W. B. Yeats

I wish first to acknowledge my debt to Henry Abramovitch for his friendship and for allowing me to use the letters and poems he sent me over the years. Some time ago we discussed the possibility of writing a book about our friendship. I hope this book fulfils that mutual dream we never managed to realise together. My warmest thanks as well to all those friends and acquaintances who inhabit this book and have enriched my life.

Over the fifty years of the Israeli occupation I have kept a journal in which I reflected on the events taking place around me and my immediate responses to them. This has enabled me to trace my emotional journey over the years and write this book.

I am grateful to my wife and life companion, Penny, for the many hours of discussion regarding this book and for being, as ever, my first reader and sternest critic. Her comments, suggestions and edits were crucial. Without her support and love through-out the many years we've been together I would not have been able to carry on with my writing.

My thanks to my UK publisher and editor, Andrew Franklin, to Carl Bromley, editorial director at The New Press, and Ben Woodward, associate editor, who worked on this manuscript with great dedication and immeasurable skill, making helpful comments and suggestions and providing much-appreciated editorial assistance. I salute their commitment to the spirit of this book.

My thanks to all the book designers, publicity direc-tors and staff at Profile Books and The New Press for their hard work in producing and promoting this book.

My thanks to my literary agent, Karolina Sutton, for her support and to George Lucas for putting me in touch with The New Press.

As with several of my other books, Lesley Levene did the copy-editing with her usual amazing profes-sionalism and sharp eye for inconsistencies and errors. I thank her warmly.

I am also grateful to my uncle Fuad and cousins Nadeem and Kareem Shehadeh and other partners at the Shehadeh Law Office, who took over a heavy load of legal work and made it possible for me to find the time to write this book.